T0302009

China's Economy in Transformation under the New Normal

EAI Series on East Asia

ISSN: 2529-718X

Series Editors: WANG Gungwu
(East Asian Institute, National University of Singapore)

ZHENG Yongnian
(East Asian Institute, National University of Singapore)

About the Series

EAI Series on East Asia was initiated by the East Asian Institute (EAI) (http://www.eai.nus.edu.sg). EAI was set up in April 1997 as an autonomous research organisation under a statute of the National University of Singapore. The analyses in this series are by scholars who have spent years researching on their areas of interest in East Asia, primarily, China, Japan and South Korea, and in the realms of politics, economy, society and international relations.

Published:

The Rise of the Regulatory State in the Chinese Health-care System
by QIAN Jiwei

Contemporary South Korean Economy: Challenges and Prospects
by CHIANG Min-Hua

China's Economy in Transformation under the New Normal
edited by Sarah Y TONG and WAN Jing

EAI Series on
East Asia

China's Economy in Transformation under the New Normal

Sarah Y TONG

WAN Jing

East Asian Institute
National University of Singapore
Singapore

NEW JERSEY · LONDON · SINGAPORE · BEIJING · SHANGHAI · HONG KONG · TAIPEI · CHENNAI · TOKYO

Published by

World Scientific Publishing Co. Pte. Ltd.

5 Toh Tuck Link, Singapore 596224

USA office: 27 Warren Street, Suite 401-402, Hackensack, NJ 07601

UK office: 57 Shelton Street, Covent Garden, London WC2H 9HE

Library of Congress Cataloging-in-Publication Data
Names: Tong, Sarah Y. (Sarah Yueting) editor. | Wan, Jing, 1981–   editor.
Title: China's economy in transformation under the new normal / [edited] by
    Sarah Y. Tong and Jing Wan, East Asian Institute, National University of Singapore.
Description: New Jersey : World Scientific, [2017] | Series: EAI series on East Asia
Identifiers: LCCN 2017016084 | ISBN 9789813208193
Subjects: LCSH: Economic development--China. | China--Economic policy--2000– |
    China--Economic conditions--2000–
Classification: LCC HC427.95 .C45626 2017 | DDC 330.951--dc23
LC record available at https://lccn.loc.gov/2017016084

British Library Cataloguing-in-Publication Data
A catalogue record for this book is available from the British Library.

Desk Editor: Dong Lixi

Typeset by Stallion Press
Email: enquiries@stallionpress.com

Printed in Singapore

Contents

List of Editors and Contributors   vii

Introduction   1
     Sarah Y TONG and WAN Jing

Chapter 1   China's Economic New Normal   7
              John WONG

Chapter 2   China's Monetary Policy in Transition   27
              Sarah CHAN

Chapter 3   China Reforms Its Social Security System   43
              LIN Shuanglin

Chapter 4   Financial Sector Reforms   65
              WAN Jing

Chapter 5   Tax Reforms in China: Recent Initiatives
              and Concerns   83
              QIAN Jiwei

Chapter 6   The Development and the Governance
              of China's Housing Development   97
              ZHOU Zhihua

Chapter 7   Private Consumption and Economic
              Restructuring   113
              CHEN Chien-Hsun

Chapter 8   Agriculture: Circulation and Management
              of Grain Reserves   127
              Jane DU

Chapter 9   The Prospect of China's Renewed State-Owned
              Enterprise Reforms   141
              Sarah Y TONG

Chapter 10   Made in China 2025: A Grand Strategy
              for Industrial Upgrading   157
              Sarah Y TONG and KONG Tuan Yuen

Chapter 11   Regional Development in China
              under Xi Jinping   171
              YU Hong

Chapter 12   China's Population Policy and the Future
              of Its Labour Market   187
              Jane DU

Chapter 13   Population Ageing and Youth Drain — Impact
              on Growth   201
              LU Ding

Index   225

List of Editors and Contributors
(Listing based on order of chapters)

Sarah Y TONG is Senior Research Fellow at the East Asian Institute, National University of Singapore. She obtained her PhD in Economics from the University of California at San Diego. Prior to joining the National University of Singapore, she held an academic position in the University of Hong Kong. Her research interests include international trade, foreign direct investment, economic reforms and industrial restructuring. Her publications have appeared in journals such as *China: An International Journal*, *China and the World Economy*, *China Economic Review*, *Global Economic Review*, *Journal of International Economics* and *Review of Development Economics*. In addition to contributing over two dozens of book chapters, she co-edited several books including *China's Great Urbanization*, published by Routledge in 2017; *China's Evolving Industrial Policy*, published by Routledge in 2014; and *China and Global Economic Crisis*, published by World Scientific in 2010. She was also editor for *Trade, Investment and Economic Integration* (vol. 2, Globalization, Development, and Security in Asia), published by World Scientific in 2014.

WAN Jing is a Visiting Research Fellow at the East Asian Institute, National University of Singapore. She obtained her PhD in Economics from the National University of Singapore. Her research interests span across various financial issues, such as analysis on stock market, capital account liberalisation, exchange rate regime reforms, shadow banking and commercial banking sector, as well as monetary policy in China. She also conducts theoretical research like endogenous business cycle and wealth distribution. Her work was recently published in *Economic Letters*.

John WONG is currently Professorial Fellow and Academic Advisor to the East Asian Institute of the National University of Singapore. He was formerly Research Director of the East Asian Institute, and Director of the Institute of East Asian Political Economy (IEAPE). Before the aforementioned appointments, he taught economics at the University of Hong Kong and subsequently at the National University of Singapore. He holds a PhD in Economics from the University of London. He has written and edited 39 books, and published numerous articles and papers on China, East Asia and ASEAN. He has also written numerous policy-related reports on development in China for the Singapore government. His first book is *Land Reform in the People's Republic of China* (New York: Praeger, 1973). His latest book is *Zhu Rongji and China's Economic Take-off* (London: Imperial College Press, 2016).

Sarah CHAN is Research Fellow at the East Asian Institute, National University of Singapore. She obtained her PhD in Economics from Nanyang Technological University. She was previously a consultant economist for the Asian Development Bank and had worked at the Monetary Authority of Singapore. Her research interests include macroeconomic developments in East Asia as well as economic policy analysis. She has published in refereed journals such as *Asian Survey*, *Asia Pacific Business Review*, *East Asian Policy: An International Quarterly*, *China: An International Journal* and *China Economic Policy Review*.

LIN Shuanglin is Professor of the National School of Development, Director of China Center for Public Finance at Peking University, and member of the Advisory Committee on Healthcare Reforms to China's State Council. He is Noddle Distinguished Professor of Economics at

University of Nebraska Omaha and Research Associate of the East Asian Institute at National University of Singapore. He obtained his Bachelor of Arts degree in Economics from Peking University, Master of Arts degree from Northwestern University and PhD in Economics from Purdue University. His research concentrates on China's public finance and economic growth. He has published extensively in academic journals, including *Journal of Economic Theory* and *Journal of Public Economics*. He has completed many research projects for China's Ministry of Finance, the World Bank and the United Nations. He is associate editor of *China Economic Quarterly*. He was president of the Chinese Economists Society 2002–2003 and chair of Department of Public Finance at Peking University 2005–2013.

QIAN Jiwei is Research Fellow at the East Asian Institute, National University of Singapore. He obtained his Bachelor of Science degree in Computer Science from Fudan University, China and PhD in Economics from the National University of Singapore. His research on Chinese health care and social policy has been published in publications such as *The China Quarterly, Health Economics, Policy and Law, Journal of Mental Health Policy and Economics, Public Administration and Development, Public Organization Review* and *Singapore Economic Review*. He has sole-authored a monograph entitled *The Rise of the Regulatory State in the Chinese Health-Care System* (Singapore: World Scientific, 2017). His current research interests include health economics, political economy and development economics.

ZHOU Zhihua is Senior Lecturer of Real Estate Economics at the Department of Architecture and the Built Environment in University of the West of England, Bristol. Prior to her academic appointment, she worked with the East Asian Institute for five years. She had worked in top property companies in China for several years before pursuing her PhD in Urban Studies at the Department of Town and Regional Planning in Sheffield University, United Kingdom. Her research interest mainly focuses on the built environment in the East Asian context, including rapid urbanisation and social transformation, housing affordability and social inequality, urban governance and regime politics, urban regeneration and class gentrification, citizen participation and community dynamics, and so on.

CHEN Chien-Hsun is a Visiting Senior Research Fellow at the East Asian Institute, National University of Singapore, and Research Fellow of the Chung-Hua Institution for Economic Research. He obtained his PhD in Economics from Oklahoma State University. He had taught at Wichita State University and formerly served as director of China Institute at Chung-Hua Institution for Economic Research. His research papers have appeared in journals such as *American Journal of Economics and Sociology, Asian Survey, China Economic Review, Economic Modelling, Eurasian Geography and Economics, Europe–Asia Studies, Journal of Comparative Economics, Journal of Contemporary Asia, Journal of Economic Policy Reform, Journal of Economic Studies, Journal of General Management, Journal of Macroeconomics, Pacific Accounting Review and Post-Communist Economies.*

Jane DU is a Visiting Research Fellow at the East Asian Institute, National University of Singapore. She completed her PhD in Economics in the University of London. Her research has two main strands: the political economy of agriculture in post-Mao China; and the economic history of structural transformation from land-based economy to capital-based economy with reference to East Asian economies. She is currently working on two books on agricultural economics of China.

KONG Tuan Yuen is a Visiting Research Fellow at the East Asian Institute, National University of Singapore. He earned his PhD in Industrial Economics from the National Central University, Taiwan. His postdoctoral fellowship at the Research Centre for Taiwan Economic Development provided him the opportunities to undertake Taiwan's economic research projects. He had also contributed actively to the Center of Southeast Asian Studies in Taiwan that holds the largest research community of Southeast Asia. He also had corporate experience in business management, financial and planning analysis at Epson, a Japanese multinational enterprise in Malaysia. His current research interests include China's industry development, especially strategic emerging industries, and China–ASEAN relations. He had published his works in *Review of Global Politics*, *Applied Econometrics and International Development* and *Journal of Overseas Chinese* and *Southeast Asian Studies*. He also frequently contributes commentaries to Singapore's largest Chinese daily *Lianhe Zaobao* and MediaCorp's FM95.8 Capital Radio.

YU Hong is Senior Research Fellow at the East Asian Institute, National University of Singapore. His research interests cover regional economic development in China, urbanisation, the "One Belt, One Road" initiatives, the Asian Infrastructure Investment Bank, China's state-owned enterprises and railway sector reform. Dr Yu's research articles have appeared in international peer-reviewed journals such as *Journal of Contemporary China*; *Asian Survey*; *China: An International Journal*; *East Asian Policy: An International Quarterly*; *The Copenhagen Journal of Asian Studies* and *Asian Politics & Policy*. He is the single author of the monograph *Economic Development and Inequality in China: the Case of Guangdong* (London and New York: Routledge, 2011). He co-edited *China's Industrial Development in the 21st Century* (Singapore: World Scientific, 2011). His most recent book is entitled *Chinese Regions in Change: Industrial Upgrading and Regional Development Strategies* (London and New York: Routledge, 2015). He also serves as a reviewer for international journals on Asian and industrial studies, including the *Journal of Contemporary China, Energy Policy, China: An International Journal, East Asian Pollicy, China Perspectives and Journal of Infrastructure Policy and Development*. He is frequently interviewed by international and local media such as Phoenix Television and *The Business Times* for his expertise on a wide range of topics.

LU Ding is Professor of Economics at the University of the Fraser Valley, Canada. He has also been affiliated with the East Asian

Institute (Singapore) as a visiting senior research fellow and Xi'an International University (China) as a special-term professor. A graduate from China's Fudan University, he obtained his PhD in Economics from Northwestern University. Before joining his current institution, he was on the faculties of Sophia University at Tokyo (2005–2008), National University of Singapore (1992–2005) and University of Nebraska at Omaha (1991–1992). He served as president of the Chinese Economists Society (North America) in 2011–2012. His research interests include regional economic development, international trade and investment, and comparative economic systems. He has published dozens of papers in professional journals, authored and edited eight academic volumes, and written book chapters in dozens of academic works. Most of his publications involve development issues in Asia-Pacific, particularly the Chinese economy.

Introduction

Sarah Y TONG and WAN Jing*

After nearly three decades of rapid growth since the late 1970s, China's economy is now the world's second largest by nominal gross domestic product (GDP) and is the world's largest by purchasing power parity (PPP) according to the International Monetary Fund (IMF).

In 1978, when Chinese economy stagnated from years of complete state control of productive resources and ineffective central planning, the government embarked on a major programme of economic reform. In an effort to reinvigorate the economy, it introduced economic incentives into the state sector, encouraged the development of rural enterprises and private businesses, liberalised foreign trade and investment, relaxed state control of prices, and increased investment in consumer-related industrial production and in education of its labour force. China achieved remarkable rapid economic growth as a result. Between 1978 and 2015, China's per capita GDP grew from US$153 to US$6,416, while its current account surplus increased by over 50 times between 1982 and 2015, from US$5.7 billion to US$293 billion.

---

* Sarah Y TONG is Senior Research Fellow at the East Asian Institute, National University of Singapore. WAN Jing is Visiting Research Fellow at the same institute.

However, such hyper growth is bound to end and since 2011, China investment-driven and export-oriented growth has decelerated to less than 7% in recent years. Various factors have contributed to China's economic slowdown. Domestically, the important concerns are mostly structural issues within the economy.

The first is the structural changes of China's population. After more than 30 years of population control programmes, China's population has been ageing at a rapid rate; the country has largely exhausted its demographic bonus, resulting in a spike in the cost of labour. The second is its highly skewed industrial structure. China has for decades relied heavily on the manufacturing sector, being highly export-oriented and reputed as the world's factory. As external demand weakens, the government highlights the need to transform the economy towards one that is domestic consumption-driven and to encourage the development of service sectors. The third is the structural problem of financing. China's investment relies primarily on indirect financing, which results in an unhealthy high leverage for both local governments and for businesses.

Externally, economic growth is constrained by uncertainties and rising protectionist tendencies. Consequently, China's long-term outlook for growth will continue to be under strong downward pressures and a relatively slower growth will likely persist in what has been termed the "New Normal". China will need to embark on a new course of structural reforms to sustain a healthy development of the economy in order to transform the country into a moderately prosperous society.

These structural reforms, first and foremost, aim for enhancement and improvement of its macroeconomic management, in particular its fiscal and monetary policies. This is essential to providing a strong support for difficult reforms and the necessary economic restructuring. Years of expansionary fiscal policy have significantly facilitated China's infrastructure construction and rapid economic growth, while strong fiscal stimulus has resulted in large accumulation of government debts, causing deep concerns over China's fiscal sustainability and long-run growth prospect. Indeed, China's government debt has become very large, both in total amount and in relation to the economy size. As a result, the government has geared towards a more precautionary fiscal policy; the current administration of Xi Jinping and Li Keqiang has pledged to keep budget deficits and government debt at manageable levels, setting the budget deficit at 3% of GDP for 2017, lower than those of recent years.

Besides fiscal policy, monetary policy plays an important role in macroeconomic and financial stability, helps promote effective financial intermediation and acts to buffer the economy against domestic and external shocks. An effective monetary policy, combined with a smooth monetary transmission mechanism, is key to the health of the economy. Meanwhile, as the financial environment becomes increasingly complex, new challenges emerge in the development and implementation of monetary policy. It is therefore imperative for China to transform its monetary policy framework from quantity-based to price-based.

Second, the role of the state in the economy should be better defined. Simply put, the fine line between the state and the market needs to be clarified. Generally speaking, state-owned enterprises (SOEs) are less productive than non-SOEs. Excessive state intervention in economic activities also increases business cost and damages firms' overall competitiveness. Much efforts have been devoted to reconfiguring the relationship between the state and the market, and reducing the state's direct involvement in business activities.

One such effort is to place more emphasis on SOE reforms. However, China's new round of SOE reforms is fraught with uncertainties. The conceptual dilemma of the role of the SOEs remains unresolved. As SOE conglomerates become larger and more influential with entrenched interest groups, any serious reform will become operationally difficult and politically risky. Furthermore, since China's SOEs are under the management of many different organs and at different levels of government, reforms can easily be sidetracked by either bureaucratic infighting or indifference.

Third, China needs to cultivate new sources for growth. Moving from an investment-driven and export-oriented growth model towards one that relies more on domestic consumption and technology and innovation will be extremely challenging. The government is committed to lead the transformation by promoting consumption, supporting research and development activities and nurturing the development of various high-tech industries. As such, domestic consumption has already become an important force to sustain growth. The government's promotion of "mass entrepreneurship and innovation" strategy as put forward by Premier Li Keqiang in 2014 had achieved encouraging outcome. For the first 10 months of 2016, year-on-year growth in certain sectors had achieved close to or over 10%; these sectors include high-tech industry (11%), equipment manufacturing industry (9%) and strategic emerging industries (11%). During the same period, investment in high-tech and service industries had reached 16% and 11%, respectively, higher than that in other industrial sectors. The government is also promoting a "Go Global" strategy to facilitate production capacity cooperation under its Belt and Road Initiatives.

In the long run, China's economic growth will be subject to various constraints and its sustainability faces mounting challenges. The most serious one is an ageing population. Unlike other issues, the framework of demographic pattern needs time to build and it is very difficult to alter people's lifestyle due to the strict implementation of the one-child policy. This is demonstrated by the less than warm response to the relaxation of the one-child policy.

Another constraint that hinders economic growth is the rising inequality in income and in wealth. Inequalities across regions and population have long been a major source of social anxiety and instability, thus obstructing efforts to stimulate consumption and transform to a more domestic consumption-driven economy. As large income gaps and societal division become entrenched, efforts to move the country towards a more innovation-driven and moderately prosperous society will be hampered.

Meanwhile, sustainable development will be further constrained by the depletion of non-renewable resources and environmental degradation. The development of environmentally friendly technologies and resource-saving industries will be challenging but rewarding. Efforts in such areas will also be the key to China's long-term sustainable development.

As a large and dynamic country, China's economic development and transformation involves many important aspects; this volume touches upon a number of key areas. The first five chapters provide an overall assessment of China's economic dynamics and deal with major macroeconomic management issues. In Chapter 1, the author examines the context underlining China's economic deceleration and emphasises the importance of its transformation. Chapter 2 reviews China's evolving monetary policy and illustrates the need to move from a quantity-based to a price-based policy framework. Focusing on China's social security, Chapter 3 analyses the system's key features, main existing problems and possible ways of reforms. Chapter 4 provides a comprehensive overview of China's reforms of its banking sector, stock market, bonds market and exchange rate regime since 2013. Chapter 5 evaluates China's tax reforms in recent years. It also highlights the several challenges in taxation, such as slower growth in tax revenue and structural imbalances between central and local governments.

The following chapters deal with important issues affecting China's economic transformation and long-term development. Chapter 6 looks at the development and governance of China's housing development. It surveys the performance of China's housing market, identifies the sector's various problems such as speculation and unaffordability in high-tier cities and high inventories in low-tier regions.

Chapter 7 concentrates on the issues of private consumption and economic restructuring. It shows that boosting private consumption is key to economic restructuring and China's future growth. Chapter 8 examines China's food security issue. It examines in particular the country's strategic grain reserve management, the major policy instrument to fulfil China's recent food security objective.

Chapter 9 assesses China's renewed SOE reforms. It examines recent policy initiatives since 2013 and highlights areas of progress and contradictions, as well as future challenges. Chapter 10 emphasises the government's Made in China 2025 programme to upgrade China's industries. It explores the importance and implications of this ambitious plan and assesses the difficulties faced by the country. Chapter 11 reviews the development of China's regional development priorities. It asserts that biased regional development policies favouring coastal regions have widened regional economic disparity and a new direction is needed.

Chapter 12 considers China's population policy and implications for its labour market. Although China has the world's largest population, labour shortage has nonetheless become an occasional problem. Swift and strong policy efforts are needed to solve China's labour market problem. Chapter 13 examines the problems of population ageing and youth drain, and assesses their impact on growth. It highlights several key demographic challenges to growth, such as shrinking working-age population and a rapid ageing society, and emphasises the imperative of industrial upgrading.

Chapter 1

China's Economic New Normal

John WONG*

High Growth Coming to an End

China's economy has experienced spectacular performance since its economic reform and the open-door policy in 1978, growing at an average annual rate of 9.7% during the 1979–2014 period, and about 10% for the two subperiods of 1991–2014 and 2001–2014.[1] Its growth was barely affected by the 1997 Asian financial crisis. Neither did it suffer much from the 2008 global financial crisis, which brought most economies to grief. In fact, China's economic growth in 2009, following the government's injection of a massive stimulus package of four trillion yuan, remained at 9.2% and quickly bounced back to 10.4% in 2010, leading the global economy to recovery. In a sense, China's long streak of high growth performance is simply historically unprecedented (Figure 1).

China's growth has started to decelerate in recent years primarily due to structural problems and the less conducive global economic environment, with 2014 registering only 7.4% growth. For 2015, growth was originally targeted at 7% but ended up at a still lower 6.9%, the lowest in 25 years. Growth in the first two quarters of 2016 registered only

---

*John WONG is Professorial Fellow at the East Asian Institute, National University of Singapore.

[1] *2015 China Statistical Abstract*, Beijing.

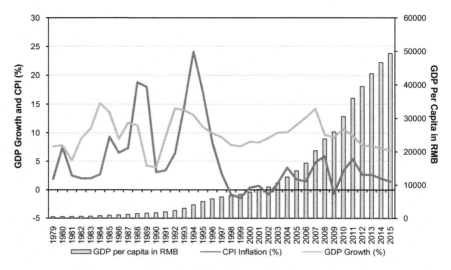

Figure 1: China's GDP, CPI and Economic Growth

Source: National Bureau of Statistics.

6.7%, indicating that growth has further come down, though apparently stabilising for a while. As the long-term outlook on growth is still under strong downward pressures, the slowdown as a process is set to continue and sustain.

In other words, China's economy has already lost its former high growth momentum and is heading for a lower and lower growth in a gradual manner. Viewed from a different perspective, China's present "lower" growth is "low" only in China's own terms as its current level of growth at around 6.7% for such a huge economy of about U$11 trillion is still remarkably high by any regional or global standard, and certainly well above the International Monetary Fund's (IMF) average global economic growth of 3.3% for 2015.

No economy can keep growing at such high rates without running into various constraints. China has chalked up double-digit rates of hyper growth for well over three decades, historically much longer than what other high-performing East Asian economies of Japan, South Korea, Taiwan, Hong Kong and Singapore had experienced before — just a little over two decades of such high growth for Japan, Korea and Taiwan, and a bit shorter for Hong Kong and Singapore. As can be seen from Table 1, Japan experienced such high growth mainly in the 1950s and the 1960s, followed by Hong Kong, South Korea, Taiwan and Singapore after the mid-1960s, the whole of the 1970s and then much of the 1980s. Malaysia and Thailand also had high growth, but not nearly as high and lasting, while India's growth performance was even more lacklustre.

China has been most remarkable for sustaining such high growth for so long. This is partly because China had enjoyed some latecomer's advantages in terms of reaping the technological backlog, but mainly because it had far greater internal dynamics in terms of having much bigger hinterlands along with a larger labour force, as compared to that of other East Asian economies. Still, after its catch-up phase of phenomenal hyper growth, China's growth must come down due to the inevitable weakening of its various growth-inducing drivers or technically, the drying up of its sources of growth.

Weakening of the Main Growth Drivers

From general economic development perspective, the major impetus of China's growth, on the supply side, is associated with the transfer of its surplus rural labour from low-productivity agriculture to higher-productivity manufacturing, a-la Arthur Lewis.[2] However such growth potential has been rapidly exhausted in recent years. China's population of age group 15–64 had started to peak in 2010 at 74.5%, with the labour supply coming near to the so-called "Lewis Turning Point". Although these potentially bad demographics have yet to be translated into immediate labour shortages, it does imply that China has already spent most of its "demographic dividend" and started to lose its comparative advantage in a wide range of labour-intensive manufacturing

---

[2] This is the central argument of the two-sector model by Nobel Laureate, W Arthur Lewis. See his book, *The Theory of Economic Growth*, London, Allen & Unwin, 1955.

Table 1: East Asia Economic Indicators

Countries	Population (Mn) 2013	GDP Per Capita (US$) 2013	Total GDP (US$ Bn) 2012	Growth of GDP (%)							
				1960–70	1970–80	1980–90	1990–2000	2000–2010	2011	2012	2013
China	1,362	6,747	8,252	5.2	5.5	10.3	9.7	10.3	9.2	7.8	7.7
Japan	127	38,491	5,984	10.9	4.3	4.1	1.3	1.1	-0.7	2.2	1.5
South Korea	50	24,382	1.151	8.6	10.1	8.9	5.7	4.2	2.4	2.7	2.8
Taiwan	23	20,980	455	9.2	9.7	7.9	5.7	3.9	1.1		2.2
Hong Kong	7.2	37,775	258	10	9.3	6.9	3.8	4.6	5.0	1.8	2.9
ASEAN-10											
Brunei	0.4	39,942	16.9	—	—	—	2.1	1.5	1.9	2.7	1.9
Cambodia	15.1	1,075	14.3	—	—	—	6.4	7.9	6.9	6.5	7.0
Indonesia	243	3,590	894	3.9	7.2	6.1	3.8	5.2	6.5	6	5.8
Laos	6.7	1,476	9.3	—	—	—	6.1	7.1	8.0	8.3	8.3

Malaysia	30.2	10,547	307	6.5	7.9	5.3	6.5	5.5	5.1	4.4	4.7
Myanmar*	53.3	868	54	—	—	—	6.1	10.8	5.5	—	5.5
Philippines	99.5	2,790	2,407	5.1	6.0	1.0	3.3	4.9	3.7	4.8	6.8
Singapore	5.4	54,710	268	8.8	8.3	6.7	7.4	5.9	4.9	2.1	4.9
Thailand	64.1	5,674	377	8.4	7.1	7.6	3.8	4.9	0.1	5.6	2.9
Vietnam	89.7	1,901	138	—	—	—	7.3	7.4	5.6	5.1	5.3
India	1,243	1,615		4.4	3.1	5.2	6.5	7.5	6.9	5.4	4.7

*Myanmar GDP data are estimates based on 2006.

Source: CIA Fact Book.

activities. *Pari passu* with its labour force decline has been the exhaustion of its easy productivity gains from early market reforms and institutional reorganisation, and technological progress embodied in the imported machines and new equipment. Hence the hyper growth has to come to an end.

In terms of contribution to growth, China's economic growth since the early 1990s has been basically driven by total domestic demand, with domestic investment playing a relatively more important role than domestic consumption. This necessarily follows that the contribution of external demand (or net exports) to China's GDP growth has all along been quite negligible in gross terms, mostly around 5% in the 1990s and then up to around 15% in recent years. During the global financial crisis as China's exports plunged, the contribution of external demand to overall GDP growth even became negative. It had remained negative in the last few years, turning slightly positive only in 2014. In fact, of the 7.4% growth in 2014, consumption accounted for 3.8% and investment 3.0% while net exports only 0.6% (Figure 2).

It thus appears that the export sector has not directly generated much GDP for China, particularly since China's exports carry high

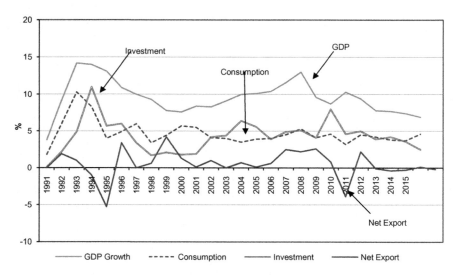

Figure 2: Sources of China's Economic Growth, 1990–2015

Source: National Bureau of Statistics.

import contents with around 50% of China's exports being processing trade. This is because China has been the base for numerous regional and global production networks and supply chains whose finished products usually contain a lot of imported materials and components, thereby netting only a small amount of domestic value-added for China. The classical example was the much publicised case of a China-assembled iPad from Apple that was sold in the US market for US$499, but yielding only US$8 to Chinese labour.[3]

However, the actual economic importance of Chinese exports to its economic growth has been seriously understated by this first-order simple analysis of gross export figures because it has missed out a lot of important "indirect" economic activities and spillovers that are connected to China's export industries if we should go for more detailed inter-sectoral analysis. Most export-oriented industries have extensive economic linkages created by various local supporting service activities as well as investment in the upstream and downstream sectors. There are also the multiplier effects on the economy generated by the spending of millions of workers and employees in the export sector.

With rising operating costs and increasing wages, China's export competitiveness for labour-intensive exports is bound to suffer.[4] The sharp rise of China's unit labour cost in recent years has been widely reported, following its double-digit rates of wage hike. According to official data, the annual average wage of all employees had increased 5.5 times for the past 13 years from 9,330 yuan in 2000 to 51,470 yuan in 2013. Minimum wages had also risen at double-digit rates for the past five years from 2010 to 2015.[5] This, along with the gradual appreciation of the renminbi (which has appreciated over 35% against the US dollar

---

[3] For the assembling of an iPhone in China, which sold for US$179 but created a total value-added of only US$6.5 in China, see Xing Yuqing, "How the iPhone Widens US Trade Deficits with China: The Story of US$6.5 Value-Added to China for its Exports of US$179", *EAI Background Brief*, no. 629, 27 May 2011.
[4] See HKTDC's report, "An Update on Production Costs on the Mainland", 12 January 2012.
[5] "China to Achieve Minimum Wage Growth Targets", *China Daily*, 29 May 2015.

since July 2005), had seriously eroded China's comparative advantage in its export markets. Consequently, China is now facing the same problem of "shifting comparative advantage" that had previously plagued Japan, South Korea and Taiwan. China would soon realise that its export sector is generating less and less growth potential for its economy. Accordingly, exports will no longer be a dependable engine of China's growth in the long run, not to mention that exports have often been the transmission mechanism of external risks and instability.

This leaves domestic investment and domestic consumption as the principal drivers of China's future growth. It is well known that China's past GDP growth has been largely investment-led. Apart from infrastructure development, industrial upgrading and housing construction are the two other major components of fixed assets investment. To cope with the 2008 global financial crisis, Premier Wen Jiabao had hastily put up a huge stimulus package of four trillion yuan to pump-prime the economy, subsequently leading to serious overinvestment as well as an overheated property market. Fixed investment had since come down substantially on account of industrial overcapacity (particularly serious for large industries like steel, cement and ferrous metals with over 20% excess capacities) and a downturn in the property market (real estate accounting for a quarter of total fixed investment). With domestic investment as the main engine of growth rapidly decelerating, GDP growth must also slow down.

Still more, the Chinese economy has been plagued by serious macroeconomic imbalance due to chronic overinvestment and under-consumption, which has led to overproduction and over-export, and eventually persistent trade surplus. In this way, China's macroeconomic imbalance has also contributed to global macroeconomic imbalances. The root cause of this unique problem is China's phenomenally high saving rate, which has been, until recently, staying close to 50%.[6]

---

[6]The basic macroeconomic identity I = S can self-explain overinvestment and over-consumption. Trade surplus can also be easily explained by another simple identity: X-M = S-I, that is, "trade surplus" as the difference between exports (X) and imports (M) equals "saving surplus", as gross savings (S) minus gross investment (I).

China's high national savings mainly come from its high household as well as high state-enterprises savings. Every year, the state has to mobilise such massive domestic savings for capital investment, from building infrastructure and housing to the technological upgrading of key manufacturing industries. Heavy capital investment had therefore been the foundation of China's past pro-growth development strategy. However the same strategy had also resulted in its unbalanced growth, with by far too much investment along with too little consumption. Hence the resulting phenomenon of overinvestment and excess capacities, one of the key factors responsible for the lower growth in 2015.

It may be argued that China's past pro-growth development strategy of "grow first, distribute later" has been the underlying cause of China's persistent phenomenon of high investment and low consumption. Other East Asian economies from Japan and Korea to Taiwan had also followed similar patterns of investment and consumption before. However such continuing investment-driven growth mode is clearly unsustainable in the long run. Specifically for China, as its population ages, its domestic saving rates are bound to decline over time as is already happening in Japan now. Viewed from a different angle, the fact that consumption is presently not the main driver of China's economic growth also means that it will be an untapped source of its future growth.

Less Obsessed with GDP-dominated Growth

Back in 1979, Deng Xiaoping launched economic reform to maximise economic growth for China, as manifested in the slogan: "To get rich is glorious". China's policymakers have since pursued such high growth strategy, almost at all costs. This had produced double-digit rates of growth for over three decades, with China's per capita GDP in 2015 about 100 times more than that in 1979. However, such a blatant GDP pursuit (dubbed "GNPism") had also generated a lot of social costs, ranging from high income inequality (with Gini ratio at 0.47 for 2014) to such undesirable by-products and negative externalities as serious air and water pollution.

This gave the new leadership under Xi Jinping an opportunity to make a decisive departure from China's time-honoured GDP-dominated pro-growth policy. Thus, China's National Bureau of Statistics (NBS), which compiles China's GDP accounts, recently declared that it had taken steps to end what it called "GDP supremacy". It had radically revised its conventional GDP accounting to give higher weights to the "quality aspects" of GDP growth like innovation and R&D, and to factor in more welfare-aspects of economic growth like the social costs of pollution. NBS also announced that it would provide a more comprehensive and multifaceted assessment of China's growth performance beyond GDP. In future, along with the release of GDP data, NBS would also provide some 40 or so core indicators that can better capture China's real economic and social changes, particularly in such crucial areas as industrial upgrading, technological development, environmental protection, rural-urban income gap, urbanisation, people's livelihood and so on.[7] This clearly implies that China's future economic growth performance will not be epitomised by changes of just one GDP indicator alone.

Finance Minister Lou Jiwei, at the 2014 G20 Finance Ministers Meeting in Cairns (September 2014) confirmed that China had indeed intended to downgrade pure GDP growth in formulating its economic policy and policy response. China's macroeconomic policy would in future focus more on comprehensive targets like stable growth, employment, inflation and so on. More significantly, the government would stick to the long-term goals of structural reforms and industrial upgrading, and would not, by and large, be distracted by short-term changes in certain GDP indicators.[8]

In broad principle, as economic growth fluctuates in future, the Chinese government is supposed to refrain from taking hasty stimulus measures just to artificially boost short-term GDP growth. In practice, however, the Chinese government has remained highly averse to any

---

[7] "Chinese Statisticians to Broaden Focus from GDP", *China Daily*, 12 September 2014 and "New Accounting Regime Ends 'GDP Supremacy'", *China Daily*, 22 September 2014.
[8] "China Will Not Alter Economic Policy", *China Daily*, 22 September 2014.

sharp volatility, be it in the stock market, economic growth or employment. As the government tends to maintain reasonably stable growth for the sake of social stability, it will still be very much inclined to step in once a serious crisis is developing, as evidenced in the heavy government intervention to save the Shanghai stock market in July 2015.

In any case, given its long central planning mindset and legacies, the Chinese government is admittedly still not fully adjusting itself to the hard reality of balancing its intended reform progress with the uncertain prospect of securing stable growth. Thus, Premier Li Keqiang had quickly changed his initially more market-oriented macroeconomic policies to become highly interventionist in terms of openly boosting growth to 7% as the growth outlook in the early part of 2015 became very gloomy. Much as what Premier Zhu Rongji had done to "protect economic growth at 8%" (*baoba*) in the late 1990s when China's economy was threatened by the Asian financial crisis, Li Keqiang had also taken a similar stand in "protecting his 7% growth" (*baoqi*) target for 2015.[9] However, latest developments indicate that such pro-growth policy based on excessive artificial intervention seems to have come to an end.

Embracing the New Normal by Xi Jinping

Unique among China's top leaders, President Xi Jinping clearly understands the basic economic growth logic. He has readily embraced China's slower growth as "New Normal", having realised that China's economy after over three decades of double-digit rates of growth must necessarily slow down due to its many inherent structural problems and constraints.

Addressing an APEC meeting in Beijing in November 2014, Xi openly dismissed any unwarranted worry about China's economic slowdown as something that is "actually not all that scary".[10] As he explained, "China's 7.7% growth in 2013 had added to China an increment of

---

[9] "Chinese Cabinet Expresses Confidence in Economy", *China Daily*, 9 July 2015.
[10] "Chinese President Says Risks to Economy 'Not That Scary'", *China Daily*, 9 November 2014.

GDP in one year that was equivalent to China's entire GDP of 1994". Xi himself is clearly not obsessed with simple high GDP growth partly because he has realised that China's growth at around 7.0% is not really low — an average annual growth of 7.0% would double GDP in 10 years — and partly because lower rates of growth in succeeding years could still create the same amount of GDP or economic activities. Xi has clearly grasped such simple GDP growth arithmetic that is based on the compound interest rate principle.

On 9 May 2016, *People's Daily* ran a front-page interview report of an anonymous "authoritative figure", which had widely been identified as Xi Jinping himself. Xi was openly critical of the demand stimulus policy of the State Council under Premier Li Keqiang, saying that such artificially propped-up growth based on the expansion of loans and credit (or debt-fuelled growth) would be unsustainable. Xi had made no bones about his preference for lower growth so as to concentrate more on supply-side structural reforms. Xi might not be fundamentally against the demand-driven growth strategy *per se*. To him, supply-side policies seem more effective in addressing China's existing economic problems plagued by over-supply and excess capacity.

What is even more remarkable is that Xi had taken pains to clarify the difference between "supply-side economics" as understood in the West and the "supply-side policy" that he has been advocating. The former refers to the conservative economic policy characteristic of Reaganomics while the latter is about the kind of policies targeting China's existing economic woes from excess industrial capacities to the many loss-making state enterprises. Hence the need for more structural reforms, along with the promotion of innovation, is critical to long-term economic growth.

Xi has also pointed out that China's economic growth during the next phase of structural reforms is likely to be flat, in the "L-shaped" trajectory rather than the "V-shaped" or W-shaped growth pattern, without short-term rebounds due to artificial demand stimulus. In other words, China's economic slowdown is set to continue, with the economy likely to be growing at a narrow range of around 6.5% for the next few years.

Whether future growth is trending up or down depends much on the actual outcome of the supply-side structural reforms.

In a way, Xi's New Normal of lower but more stable growth is essentially a managed economic slowdown that will also facilitate the reform and rebalancing of the economy. The government will use the stable growth environment to create more higher-quality jobs as well as carry out reform and restructuring in various areas, ranging from land and labour to local public finance and state-owned enterprises (SOEs). In the short run, reform and rebalancing could, of course, put pressures on economic growth. In the long run, however, progress in reform and restructuring should yield sufficient "reform dividend" for the economy to make a successful transition towards the "developed economy" status.

Managing the New Normal of Lower Growth

In accepting the New Normal, China needs to develop *new* sources of growth for the future. The kind of higher-quality and more efficient economic growth as conceived by Xi Jinping has to be based on opening up new sources of growth associated with (i) innovation and technological progress; (ii) deepening of market reform; and (iii) accelerating industrial restructuring. In particular, Xi has repeatedly emphasised the importance of innovation and technological progress as well as more thorough-going market reform.

For any economy, innovation and technological progress is the fundamental source of its productivity growth. China's past dynamic growth had indeed been fuelled by significant technological progress associated with imported technology and initial market reform. However, China has now exhausted such easy source of technological progress, the so-called "picking from the low-hanging trees" way; future productivity gains therefore will need to come from its own R&D efforts.

In recent years, China has rapidly expanded its R&D activities, which reached 2.1% of GDP in 2014, compared to the 2.8% for the

United States and 3.4% for Japan. In total terms, however, China's global share of R&D spending is in reality not low, being the world's second-largest after that of the United States. In 2014 alone, some 2.4 million new patents were registered in China. The "Nature Index/ Global" (which tracks the sources of publication of high-quality scientific papers) also ranks China in 2014 as having published the world's second-largest number of scientific papers after the United States. With more than seven million new university graduates every year and an industrial base that is rapidly expanding and becoming increasingly more sophisticated, China is admittedly on track to develop a viable technological base that will eventually generate new sources of productivity increases to support future economic growth. Not surprisingly, the 2014 Bloomberg Global Innovation Index ranked China as the world's 25th most innovative country (the top 20 being mostly OECD countries) in total innovation score, being the first in manufacturing rank, third in high-tech density and fourth in patent activity.

China will also face even greater challenge in capturing more productivity gains from "continuing institutional innovation" through more thorough-going market reform. Since China can no longer reap simple and easy productivity gains from its early phases of introducing the market system, its major task now is to squeeze even greater efficiency and productivity through deepening market reform, including allowing the market to play a more central role in resource allocation in the critical areas of the economy. Whereas technological innovation is the "hardware", institutional innovation through further market reform and deregulation can be considered as the "software", or just the kind of needed "supply-side policies" to boost TFP (total factor productivity) growth for the next lap of growth. All this, in turn, critically depends on the strong political will of Xi's leadership, first to initiate structural reforms and then implement the necessary changes.

At the Third Party Plenum in November 2013, Xi Jinping announced a bold and comprehensive reform package covering many critical areas such as financial sector reform, central-local fiscal relations, competition policy, SOE reform, rural land policy, foreign trade and foreign investment and so on. At the Fourth Party Plenum in October 2014, the main reform focus shifted to legal reform in order to strengthen China's "rule of law". Finally, China has come to recognise that an effective and functioning legal framework is simply indispensable for good governance, which in turn holds the key to the successful implementation of various reforms.

Xi had indeed laid out many reform plans on the table. They are all critical and are also interdependent. So far, the financial sector reform and the reform of local public finance have made good progress while the rural land reform seems to get bogged down. For SOE reform, it is admittedly difficult and involves a necessarily long-drawn-out process as too many established interests are involved. Xi has adopted a clever strategy of using his anti-corruption campaign to pry open some large SOEs for reform and reorganisation. He has already restructured the SOEs related to oil and gas, and the railway. He has since extended his target to the mass media, higher education and civil aviation. More significantly, the government has declared its intention to close down heavily loss-making zombie SOEs. Within one year, the large central-controlled SOEs dropped from 112 to 105, with five more in the process of being shut down.[11] Such reform endeavour will therefore be highly critical for the Chinese economy.

Part of China's past growth was essentially derived from the sheer injection of a massive amount of capital (basically from its high domestic savings) along with abundant cheap labour. Now as China's fertility rates have sharply declined, it has also fast exhausted its "demographic dividend" for development. This follows that the next phase of growth will all the more have to shift from dumping in more inputs to fostering higher TFP growth based on not just technological innovation but also institutional innovation like deepening and broadening of the market reform. Once the reform has achieved a significant breakthrough, China's economy would then reap the "reform dividend" for its next lap of growth.

---

[11] "Shake-up of SOEs Set to Continue", *China Daily*, 15 July 2016.

Last but not least is the need to step up industrial restructuring and upgrading. Successful East Asian economies like South Korea, Taiwan and Singapore had all started their industrialisation based on labour-intensive manufacturing. In the course of time — normally after a decade or so of intensive industrialisation — they experienced labour shortages as well as losing comparative advantage for their manufactured exports due to rising cost and increasing wages. Thus, they had to undergo their second phase of industrialisation, mainly in the late 1970s and the early 1980s, through industrial upgrading or restructuring of their industries towards more capital-intensive and higher value-added activities.

As China has basically followed such "East Asian model" of economic development based on growing manufactured exports, China will also have to undergo similar process of economic restructuring — which was called the "Second Industrial Revolution" in Singapore — which had not been a smooth-going process even for this small country. For China in recent years, its wage hike at double-digit rates is a clear manifestation of its increasingly tighter labour market while its sharply declining export growth from double- to single-digit rates is also the tell-tale sign of it losing comparative advantage for its labour-intensive manufactured exports. China's industrial upgrading is therefore long overdue.

Notably, the process of industrial upgrading had already started many years back; and it had in fact been emphasised as one of the central policy focuses in China's 11th Five-Year Plan (2006–2010). Over the years, the Guangdong government had vigorously pushed the industrial restructuring of its many small and medium labour-intensive industries in the Pearl River Delta region while the Yangtze Delta region had also undergone significant industrial upgrading towards more capital-intensive and skill-intensive activities. In the Binhai region around Tianjin, however, the main focus had been on setting up large-scale, technology-intensive new industries related to space, aircraft manufacturing, new energy, new materials and so on, with heavy state support. Overall, China's manufacturing sector has no doubt made significant achievements in moving up the value chain, as evidenced by its increasing production of those high-technology items. However, China's manufactured exports have remained basically dominated by labour-intensive products or goods with low domestic value-added.

In a truly market economy, industrial restructuring is apt to be a gradual process of structural change to be properly guided by market signals. Xi Jinping and Li Keqiang are naturally impatient with such a market driven but slow-going process. Recently, the Chinese government unveiled the "Made in China 2025" plan, which is China's first action plan (reportedly to be quite similar to Germany's "Industry 4.0" plan or its Fourth Industrial Revolution) to promote "intensive manufacturing". Its main objective is to transform China's manufacturing sector from its present stage of being just a global manufacturing giant in terms of sheer volumes and output to a leading manufacturing power of the world in a quality sense. The key jargon is to upgrade China's manufacturing industries from "Made in China" to "Created in China". To this end, the focus for the next 10 years is to achieve significant breakthroughs in 10 crucial sectors comprising information technology, numerical control tools and robotics, aerospace equipment, ocean engineering and high-tech ships, railway equipment, energy saving and new energy, power equipment, new materials, medicine and medical devices, and agricultural machinery.

Suffice it to say that the implementation of this new manufacturing Master Plan will create a powerful new growth engine that should propel China's next phase of economic growth to cross the threshold of a developed economy by 2030 and also beyond.

A Successful New Normal as a Successful Transition to a Developed Economy?

The World Bank on 27 February 2012 released a study titled, *China 2030: Building a Modern, Harmonious, and Creative High-Income Society*, which states that China has reached "a turning point in its development path". The report has also warned that "China's growth will decline gradually in the years leading to 2030 as China reaches the limits of growth brought about by current technologies and its current economic structure".

Together with China's government think tank Development Research Centre, the World Bank has done the growth trajectory made up of five discrete sets of average growth rates based on a series of China's Five-Year Plans: 9.9% growth for the 10th FYP (already achieved), 8.6% for the 11th, 7.0% for the 12th, 5.9% for the 13th and only 5.0% for the 14th (2025–2030) as shown in Table 2.

Hence, projecting into the future, China's economy by 2030 is to surpass the US economy to become the world's largest, with a total GDP of US$24.4 trillion (compared to about $17 trillion for the US economy in 2014) at current US exchange rate. This projection now looks a little too conservative for the current state of the Chinese economy, as China is clearly set to fulfil this final target well before 2030!

Table 2: China's Future Economic Structure: Projected Growth Pattern Assuming Steady Reforms and No Major Shocks (%)

Indicator	1995–2010	2011–2015	2016–2020	2021–2025	2026–2030
GDP Growth	9.9	8.6	7.0	5.9	5.0
Labour Growth	0.9	0.3	−0.2	−0.2	−0.4
Labour Productivity Growth	8.9	8.3	7.1	6.2	5.5
Structure of Economy (end of period)					
Investment/GDP	46.4	42	38	36	34
Consumption/GDP	48.6	56	60	63	66
Manufacturing/GDP	46.9	43.8	41.0	38.0	34.6
Service/GDP	43.0	47.6	51.6	56.1	61.1
Share of Employment in Agriculture	38.1	30.0	23.7	18.2	12.5
Share of Employment in Service	34.1	42.0	47.6	52.9	59.0

Source: World Bank, *China 2030: Building a Modern, Harmonious and Creative High-income Society*, 2012.

Of greater importance is the fact that against the projected population of 1.47 billion, China's per capita GDP in 2030 will be about US$16,000–17,000 at current exchange rate, which is about the level of per capita GDP of South Korea in 2005, Singapore's in 1993 or Japan's in 1970. In any case, China will by then have definitely become a "developed economy", albeit still a low-income developed economy.

There are actually no universally accepted yardsticks to define a "developed economy". Beyond the per-capita GDP level, other common economic indicators like industrialisation, infrastructure and human resource development have been used; however, they are too complicated to compare across countries. Accordingly, the World Bank has simply classified countries into four categories of low, lower middle, upper middle and high income economies on the basis of their (nominal) per-capita GDP level. For many years, the per capita GDP of US$10,000 had been used as a convenient cut-off point to categorise a country to be a "high-income economy", or a proxy for a "developed economy".

Thus, Japan's per capita GDP reached the US$10,000 level in 1965, just about 18 years from the start of its post-war high growth. Singapore reached this level in 1981, also 18 years after the beginning of its high growth in 1966. Taiwan reached this level in 1992, after about 26 years of its high growth. South Korea reached this level also in 1992, after about 25 years of its high growth. For China, its per capita GDP by early 2016 still stood at US$8,000 (ranking only at the world's 78th position) after its 35 years of continuing high growth. On account of its huge population, China's per-capita GDP level is apt to remain low even after having sustained such a long period of high growth.

If the threshold of a developed economy were to be raised to the per-capita income level of US$15,000, as implied by the World Bank projection discussed earlier, it would take China from 2016 another five or six years to reach that level assuming a continuing 7% growth; or about 10 years for a continuing 6% growth. In this context, China would certainly become a "developed economy" before 2030. However, it will still take China another long journey to become a truly affluent society that is better reflected in the much higher level of per capita

GDP. In short, a successful "New Normal" will provide the successful transition to a developed economy in future.

To Xi Jinping, the more challenging goal is admittedly the realisation of his "Chinese Dream". For this, he has aimed higher and set his long-term vision of China developing into a fully developed *fuqiang* (rich and powerful) country by 2049, or exactly 100 years after the founding of the People's Republic (the Communist Revolution) in 1949.

Chapter 2

China's Monetary Policy in Transition

Sarah CHAN*

Evolving Monetary Policy Framework

As China increasingly integrates with the global economy and becomes more open to international trade and financial flows, developing an effective monetary policy framework is particularly crucial. Monetary policy plays an important role in macroeconomic and financial stability, helps promote effective financial intermediation (i.e. allocation of resources) and acts to buffer the economy against domestic and external shocks.

China's monetary policy framework has evolved over time but financial liberalisation in recent years has changed the landscape within which monetary policy operates and poses new challenges to policy management. Further, a tightly managed exchange rate regime and an underdeveloped financial system can reduce monetary policy autonomy and the efficiency of monetary transmission mechanism.

China's current monetary policy framework is still largely characterised by quantitative and administrative management. Since the early years of China's opening up, the People's Bank of China (PBOC) has relied heavily on quantitative control of the domestic credit channel to influence economic activity. Quotas to control credit directly were

---

*Sarah CHAN is Research Fellow at the East Asian Institute, National University of Singapore.

mainly used during 1984–1997. In 1998, the PBOC abolished credit ceilings and established an indirect management framework, with stabilising and promoting economic growth as the final policy goal and monetary aggregates (M1, M2, etc.) as intermediate targets, and using mainly tools such as open market operations, reserve requirement ratio, central bank lending and rediscounting (Table 1) to regulate the monetary base. Macro-prudential measures are also employed to manage credit expansion and influence money supply.

Although the PBOC has sometimes adjusted benchmark deposit and lending rates and guided short-term movement in the interbank market, interest rates have played a much smaller role in helping to achieve the targets for monetary aggregates. Monetary policy operations still rely heavily on quantitative management to adjust money supply. Figure 1 shows the close correlation between bank lending, M2 and investment. The pick-up in 2002–03, the sharp slowdown in 2004, the surge in 2008–09 and the subsequent slowdown in real fixed assets investment were due to intentional credit adjustment. In comparison, interest rates did not move much during the mentioned episodes in the last decade.

Transmission Mechanism of Monetary Policy

The transition of China's monetary policy framework from one focusing on administrative measures and quantitative credit targets to one basing on a more market-based system faces challenges. Since 1996, the PBOC has begun its own gradual process to liberalise interest rates in the banking, capital market and local and foreign currencies segments. By 1999, the PBOC had removed all restrictions on money market and bond market rates, essentially allowing government and financial institution bonds as well as interbank lending to be priced by the market. On 26 October 2015, the PBOC announced the removal of all remaining controls on deposit rates. Despite moves to deregulate bank lending and deposit rates, implicit interest rate control still remains as the majority of state-owned enterprises (SOEs), local governments and well-connected large firms still borrow at benchmark rates, which are

Table 1: PBOC's Policy Toolkit

Tools	What is it?	Typical Duration	Aim/Objective
OMOs (Open market operations)	PBOC makes short-term collateralised loans (reverse repo)/borrowings (repo or issues central bank bills) with financial institutions to adjust reserve money supply. Regular operations now conducted on a daily basis.	Ranging from 7-day to 3-year, typically 7/14/28-day	Direct and immediate impact on the overall interbank liquidity conditions.
SLF (Standing Lending Facility)	Collateralised loans from PBOC to financial institutions that request funding. This is similar to the US Federal Reserve's discount window and the European Central Bank's marginal lending facility. It usually has one- to three-month maturity and requires collateral for providing liquidity support to financial institutions.	Typically ranging from 1 to 3 months and shorter maturity up to 14-day for small institutions	Meet relatively large liquidity needs with medium maturity.
RRR (Required Reserve Requirement)	PBOC can adjust RRR (the portion of deposits that financial institutions are required to put in PBOC) for all financial institutions or targeted group of financial institutions.	Liquidity impact permanent	Long-lasting liquidity release (when RRR is lowered) or withdrawal (when RRR is increased).

(Continued)

Table 1: (*Continued*)

Tools	What is it?	Typical Duration	Aim/Objective
PSL (Pledged Supplementary Lending)	Collateralised loans from PBOC to financial institutions for specific purposes. PSL differs from traditional re-lending used by the PBOC as a frequent liquidity management tool in that it requires collateral such as Treasury bonds and bills and has loan maturity of more than a year (while re-lending loans typically mature in less than a year). Further, the PSL's interest rate is market-determined while that of re-lending is determined by the PBOC irrespective of market conditions. So PSL is relatively more transparent than re-lending.	Typically 3-year in tenor	Long-term financial support for targeted areas (e.g. social housing); a quasi-fiscal action.
Re-lending	Major types: 1) loans to financial institutions to support certain sectors (e.g. agricultural sector, small/micro enterprises); a quasi-fiscal action; 2) loans to financial institutions for short-term liquidity needs and typically uncollateralised.	Typical maximum maturity around 1-year	1) Targeted support for underserved borrowers; 2) short-term liquidity support for commercial banks.
Bill rediscount	Commercial banks discount undue bills with PBOC in exchange for cash.	Short term	Meet liquidity need for commercial banks.
SLO (Short-term liquidity operation)	A supplement to OMO and is used on a discretionary basis to manage temporary fluctuation of liquidity in the banking system.	Very short-term, typically a few days	Meet very short-term liquidity needs.

Source: Goldman Sachs, "Global Economics Weekly", 23 May 2015.

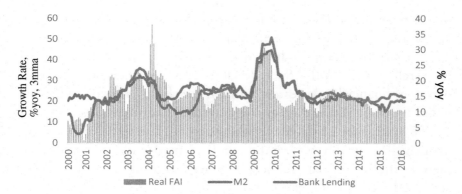

Figure 1:   Bank Credit and Real Fixed Assets Investment Growth
Source: CEIC.

typically below market rates due to financial repression.[1] The effects of
interest rate liberalisation are somewhat muted by benchmark lending
rates and indicative of hidden interest rate controls and financial distor-
tion in the credit market.

Clearly, the government's "implicit guarantee" policy and soft financial constraints (i.e. the phenomenon whereby financially insolvent
firms can avoid bankruptcy and be bailed out by funding from external
sources) diminish the role of price-based tools by making SOEs and
local governments insensitive to interest rate movements. The introduction of new policy tools, such as short-term liquidity operations
(SLO), standing lending facility (SLF) and pledged supplementary
lending (PSL) that were introduced in 2013 and 2014 to augment the
PBOC's open market operations on liquidity management, marked a
step towards the marketisation of interest rates. However, these schemes
are still determined by administrative directives as to which banks will
get liquidity injection and which sectors these banks can lend to.

The rise of shadow banking and internet finance has significantly
impaired the PBOC's monetary policy management capability. The
development of new financial offerings such as wealth management

---

[1] Chi Lo, "China's Impossible Trinity: The Structural Challenges to the 'Chinese
Dream'", 2015.

products and trust loans implies that bank deposits have declined in importance in the funding of financial intermediation and the development of shadow credit products has reduced the share of bank lending in overall credit growth.[2] Such developments have increased the complexity of financial linkages and reduced the effectiveness of traditional policy tools such as lending quotas and reserve requirements.

The emergence of shadow banking activities and off-balance sheet financing has notably made it difficult for central bank policymakers to identify the appropriate monetary aggregates to influence economic activity. It complicates the PBOC's monetary reform since financial innovation and arbitrage has made traditional monetary indicators such as money supply and bank credit growth unstable and unreliable for conducting monetary policy. The fact that financial liberalisation is ongoing while reforms of the SOEs are lagging adds another complication to monetary policy transmission as the large presence of state companies and their favoured access to credit impede the transmission of the interest-rate channel and renders monetary policy ineffective.

Further, a technical problem with reforming China's monetary policy framework is that the PBOC has too many policy targets/goals (given the transitional nature of its economy) but not enough policy instruments to deliver them. The Tinbergen rule states that each independent policy target should be delivered by at least one independent policy tool for monetary policy to be effective. If there are fewer tools than targets, then some policy goals will not be achievable. The PBOC has price stability, full employment, strong GDP growth, favourable external balance, stable exchange rate, financial stability and structural reforms as its policy goals but until recently, it only has benchmark interest rates, reserve requirements and loan quotas in its policy tool kit

---

[2]Wang Tao, "China's Evolving Monetary Policy Framework", Joint Conference by People's Bank of China and the International Monetary Fund on New Issues in Monetary Policy: International Experience and Relevance for China, 27 March 2014, <https://www.imf.org/external/np/seminars/eng/2014/pbc/pdf/Book 070214.pdf> (accessed 23 June 2016).

which are not market-based instruments.[3] The PBOC's pursuit of multiple objectives has brought challenges and also impacted the central bank's independence.[4]

Although some market discipline was introduced to the financial system with the introduction of the OMO and various lending facilities in 2013, these tools, as mentioned, are not effective in delivering the policy targets mainly because they are still distorted by administrative controls while the economy has moved on to become more market-driven.[5] Further, targeting easing through the SLO, SLF and PSL is typically conducted off the market and due to the lack of signalling effect, it sends no policy messages to the market. This suggests that the PBOC is still stuck with an outdated practice whereby central banks moved in secrecy to shock the markets in order to maximise their policy impact. Although transparency is not necessary since the PBOC is not independent of the government,[6] the lack of transparency could prevent the markets from reacting to policy decisions, undermining the effectiveness of monetary policy. The *modus operandi* of secrecy has now become obsolete as global monetary authorities realise that policy transparency through "forward guidance" is a more effective monetary management approach.

---

[3] Granted, many other central banks (like the US Federal Reserve and Bank of Japan) have multiple policy goals, they do not suffer as seriously as China from the policy-instrument goal mismatch as the latter has many more policy goals and few policy instruments than other central banks.

[4] PBOC Governor Zhou Xiaochuan said in a speech in Washington that the central bank's multiple objectives require more coordination with other government agencies; hence, it is not easy to be independent compared to a central bank which only has price stability as its sole mandate. Refer to <https://www.imf.org/external/np/speeches/2016/062416.htm> (accessed 22 July 2016).

[5] Chi Lo, "China's Impossible Trinity: The Structural Challenges to the 'Chinese Dream'", 2015.

[6] The central bank formally acts under the leadership of the State Council which approves key issues of monetary policy (i.e. the annual supply of bank notes, the setting of interest rates and exchange rate policy).

Depending on the needs of the economy, the PBOC had put vary-ing emphases on the importance of its multiple policy goals at different times in the past. For instance, when China experienced overheating or inflationary pressures from 2006 to 2008, its policy focus was on price stability, which later shifted to supporting GDP and employment growth as well as safeguarding financial stability in the aftermath of the global subprime crisis in 2008–09. The priority focus again changed to balancing economic growth and containing excessive leverage as a result of the debt overhang arising from rapid credit expansion.

A new policy goal — financial stability — has surfaced, arising from the rapidly growing shadow-banking market. Chinese banks' shadow credit, in existence since 2010, is estimated to have grown at 46% CAGR (compound annual growth rate) from 2012 to 1Q 2016 to RMB21 trillion, or 10% of total banking assets.[7] The surge in credit expansion within the financial sector poses a key macro risk as it could lead to asset bubbles and make the financial sector fragile, constraining the effectiveness of monetary policy. Chinese banks are also engineer-ing more innovative structures to bypass regulatory scrutiny on capital, provisions and underwriting standards. The authorities have moved to tighten risk controls and enhance financial regulatory reforms in order to mitigate potential systemic risks that could jeopardise the economy.

Monetary Policy Reforms and Challenges

China's benchmark policy rates have long been the one-year lending and deposit rates. In the past, policy rate adjustments would have a direct impact on money supply growth given the presence of a lending rate floor and deposit rate ceiling. However, the central bank removed the lending rate floor in July 2013 and the deposit rate ceiling in October 2015. Banks have since been able to freely price their loans and deposits. However, the central bank still announces changes to the lending and deposit rates as part of its policy framework to ensure that banks do not engage in aggressive deposit competition in the initial

---

[7] Deutsche Bank, "No More Hiding behind Shadow", 19 May 2016.

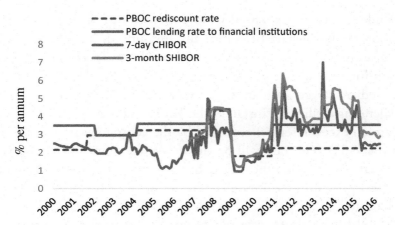

Figure 2:   PBOC Policy Rates and Money Market Rates
Source: CEIC.

phase after interest rate liberalisation. However, the central bank also recognises that the guidance value of these two rates as policy benchmarks is fading.[8] There is also little correlation between PBOC policy rates and money market rates (Figure 2). The market currently sees the 7-day repo and 3-month SHIBOR (Shanghai interbank offered rate) rates as the best indicators of interbank market liquidity and benchmarks for pricing other financial instruments.

The PBOC has started considering a new policy framework — the interest rate corridor — which has the merit of effective policy communication and monetary transmission. The interest rate corridor is a monetary management system that involves three policy rates — an interest rate ceiling, a floor and a target policy rate set by the central bank between the rate ceiling and the floor. The policy target rate is usually a short-term or overnight interest rate prevailing in the interbank market. The central bank picks the policy target rate to manage liquidity conditions and market expectations that are consistent with attaining its policy goals.

---

[8] HSBC, "China's New Policy Rate: An Introduction to the Interest Rate Corridor", 29 February 2016.

While China has expressed its intention to introduce a policy rate corridor, no details have been formally announced. Market players are already estimating that the interest rate corridor will focus on short-end market interest rates (e.g. 7-day repo and 3-month SHIBOR) as the intermediate target, with an upper bound (the interest rate on central bank lending facility, for instance, the SLF) and lower bound (the interest rate on excess reserves) managed by the central bank. It is believed that the 7-day repo rate will be the new policy rate since it shows a higher correlation than the overnight repo rate with longer-term interest rates, providing a more effective monetary policy pass-through mechanism.[9]

Establishing a short-term policy rate anchor is therefore a critical first step for the central bank to improve the transmission mechanism of monetary policy and anchor expectations. At the moment, interest rates have become more market-driven due to financial liberalisation and since mid-2013, the PBOC has begun to experiment using market-based interest rates for monetary management. As the monetary policy framework evolves within a more liberalised financial system, the focus will shift from traditional rules-based administrative and quantitative measures to a more market-based and price-based approach. As financial liberalisation gathers pace, the PBOC may have to improve and broaden its measurements of monetary aggregates (to M3, for example) as traditional monetary aggregates are getting increasingly less relevant. It also has to strengthen prudential supervision since during the transition period, some state-owned financial institutions which lack good corporate governance may become more aggressive in their risk-taking behaviour as they gain more freedom in deciding loan quantity and prices.

The establishment of an interest-rate regime is a longer-term development. Capital allocation efficiency could be improved with the introduction of an interest rate corridor by making banks more

---

[9]Nomura Asia Economic Monthly, "China's Monetary Policy Regime in Transition", 7 April 2016.

sensitive to interest rates, allowing them to make more autonomous risk-taking decisions. The corridor may also lower interest rate volatility. The volatility of short-term interest rates has increased with the growth of the interbank market (Figure 3), resulting in more interest rate fluctuations and reflecting more complicated interbank market activities involving more diverse participants, more complex financial products and more sophisticated liquidity management practices. This poses new challenges to managing liquidity and implementing monetary policy. With a credible interest rate corridor system, the PBOC will have more means to manage liquidity conditions and market expectations and reduce excessive interest rate volatility.

For a large economy like China with a high degree of domestic orientation, the need for an independent monetary policy to deal with domestic and external shocks is crucial. Hence, having an independent monetary policy is important for overall macroeconomic stability. In China, the main nominal anchor for monetary policy has been the nominal exchange rate, which was pegged to the dollar from the mid-1990s until July 2005. The dollar peg was abandoned for a "managed floating" exchange rate in 2005 but reinstituted in the wake of the global financial crisis in July 2008 until 2010 when the renminbi (RMB) was subsequently managed against an undisclosed basket of currencies. In practice, the RMB was tightly managed against the dollar

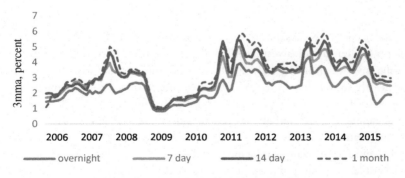

Figure 3:   Collateralised Repo Rates (%)

Source: CEIC.

with very limited flexibility; mounting evidence suggests that China faces an increasing challenge to maintaining monetary autonomy and the stability of the RMB given the substantial relaxation of capital controls over the years.[10]

Suffice it to say that as the capital account becomes increasingly open and amidst the government's desire to push forward RMB internationalisation, China will find it increasingly difficult to use interest rate tools to manage the economy and maintain exchange rate stability. The PBOC's inability to use interest rates as a primary tool of monetary policy implies that monetary growth has to be controlled by blunt and non-market-oriented instruments such as targets or ceilings for credit growth and "non-prudential administrative measures". For most of the past decade, the PBOC had been able to retain some degree of monetary autonomy by sterilising capital inflows to mitigate the inflationary effect of excess money supply (the huge accumulation of foreign exchange reserves has resulted as a consequence of foreign exchange market intervention to counter the appreciation of the yuan). Although the PBOC encounters a great demand for its bills even at relatively low interest rates — a result of both high savings rates in the private and corporate sectors as well as limited diversification opportunities in the capital market — sterilisation proved to be costly and also unsustainable.

In the context of capital outflows, the challenge of maintaining monetary autonomy and exchange rate stability has become greater.[11]

---

[10]Capital account liberalisation has progressed gradually from loosening of restrictions on foreign direct investment (FDI) in the early 1990s to liberalisation of portfolio investment in the early 2000s, starting from institutional investment and subsequently to individual investors. Although the process was interrupted in 1997 by the Asian financial crisis and the 2008–09 global financial crisis, deregulation of China's capital account transactions has gained momentum since 2010 along with RMB internationalisation.

[11]There would be less scope to use independent monetary policy if the exchange rate is not flexible. Over most of the past decade, the PBOC was a net purchaser of FX as both the current and capital accounts were in surplus. The purchases not only increased PBOC's reserves but were also the main conduit of expanding base money. When capital outflows dried up FX purchases and PBOC has to sell reserves to

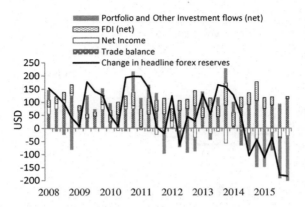

Figure 4: **Change in Foreign Exchange Reserves and Balance of Payments**
Source: CEIC.

Although the PBOC widened the onshore trading band for the RMB in 2012 and subsequently in 2014 to make the exchange rate more flexible, this on its own does not represent a very significant change to PBOC's exchange rate management. As the exchange rate still remains tightly managed, efforts to ease monetary policy have been less effective because of FX (forex) leakages; in the face of persistent capital outflow pressures since 2014 (Figure 4), the PBOC has had to neutralise the liquidity impact by resorting to domestic liquidity injection instruments including open market operations and repeatedly cutting banks' RRRs in order to maintain adequate liquidity (Figure 5).

The implication that emerges is that of a heavily constrained monetary policy framework where the nominal exchange rate remains the key nominal anchor and a variety of mostly quantitative tools are used to implement monetary policy. As monetary policy independence is too important to be relinquished, China has to enhance exchange rate flexibility in order to aid monetary policy management. However, China's policymakers face a major conundrum given the Impossible

---

defend the exchange rate, it has the adverse impact of reducing base money supply or tightening monetary conditions unless measures like reverse repos and RRR cuts were taken to neutralise the liquidity impact.

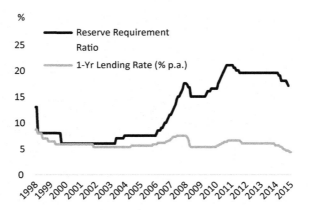

Figure 5: RRR and Interest Rate

Source: CEIC.

Trinity trilemma — there will be less scope for monetary autonomy if the exchange rate is tightly managed and the capital account is further liberalised. In addition, RMB internationalisation requires a more flexible exchange rate regime and the RMB needs to be "freely usable" now that it is included in the International Monetary Fund's Special Drawing Rights basket.

With China experiencing slower economic growth and the real interest rate remaining elevated,[12] monetary policy needs to be accommodative. Since mid-2012, the PBOC has been mainly using repo or reverse repo auctions to manage liquidity conditions and signal its monetary policy intentions. The government reportedly stated that it will maintain a "prudent" monetary policy (i.e. policy will be kept "neither too tight nor too loose") and has used targeted bank-RRR cuts on selective banks to fine-tune base money growth and ease credit constraints. It also removed the 75% loan-to-deposit ratio cap in 2015 to deregulate the banking system and free up liquidity to boost lending.

---

[12] The PBOC's multiple rate cuts since 2014 have lowered nominal interest rates but the real interest rates faced by companies remain high — the weighted average bank lending rate minus PPI inflation reached 5.6% in 1Q 2016.

To address downside risks to growth, the government would have to combine monetary policy with fiscal and supply-side reforms to strike a balance between supporting GDP growth, restructuring the economy and managing inflationary expectations.[13]

Conclusion

As the Chinese economy becomes more developed and market-oriented, market-based monetary policies are needed to enhance macroeconomic stability. The PBOC's quantitative-based approach to targeting money supply has the disadvantage of causing interest rate volatility in the interbank market to be typically higher in China than in countries with an implementation framework based around an overnight policy interest rate. Making frequent use of price-based tools (i.e. interest rates) would reduce not only short-term interest rate volatility, but also the PBOC's reliance on changes in required reserves as a means of controlling liquidity, which in general risk becoming less effective as other forms of financial intermediation outside the banking system gain prominence. Further, it would lessen the PBOC's reliance on "window guidance" to commercial banks which weakens competition and undermine the market determination of interest rates.

Further interest rate reform will need to be carried out by changes in currency market arrangements given the constraints on monetary policy effectiveness. The PBOC is expected to promote reforms of the exchange rate regime in a gradual and coordinated manner, with a view to maintaining monetary policy independence. In the shift to a full-fledged market-based monetary policy regime, it will also have to make

---

[13] Fiscal policies have to complement monetary policy to support growth. Since 2008, the government has relied on monetary policy to stabilise growth several times but the efficiency of this strategy is clearly declining. Between 2008 and mid-2014, the new credit extended by banks had helped to form almost equal amount of new money supply. In contrast, since July 2014, every RMB100 new credit extended by banks has only resulted in around RMB60 increase in M2. Deutsche Bank, "China Tail Risk Series III: Hidden Risks in the Financial Sector", 5 May 2016.

monetary policy more forward-looking and anticipatory as well as deepen banking and financial sector reform. Regulatory supervision will also need to be strengthened to keep up with financial innovation. Ultimately, China's economy can only develop and achieve sustainable growth if monetary policies become market-determined within a gradually liberalised financial sector.

Chapter 3

China Reforms Its Social Security System

LIN Shuanglin*

An Indispensable Reform

One of the most pressing issues in China is social security reform. China's urban social security system, established in the early 1950s, features a large unfunded defined-benefit social pooling account, which is pay-as-you-go (PAYG) in nature, and a small funded defined-contribution personal account.[1]

In 2009 China established a rural social security system. Young farmers contribute a small amount of funds to their personal accounts

---

*LIN Shuanglin is Professor at China Centre for Public Finance, National School of Development in Peking University and Noddle Distinguished Professor at Department of Economics, College of Business Administration, University of Nebraska Omaha.
[1] With a defined-benefit social security system, a worker makes agreed-upon contributions to the social retirement plan and receives agreed-upon benefits upon retirement. With a defined-contribution system, a worker can contribute to a private account, with or without the employer's contribution. When retired, the worker receives whatever remains in the private account. With a funded social security system, the present value of benefits received should be equal to the contributions made by an individual. With an unfunded social security system, the present value of benefits received by the retiree may not be equal to the total contributions made by the person.

with some government subsidies, while their parents receive a small amount of retirement benefits financed by general government revenue. Nearly all farmers were covered by the rural social security system. Recently China had established a similar social security system for non-working urban residents.

China faces a severe problem of population ageing because of the birth control policy adopted in the early 1970s and the one-child policy adopted in the early 1980s. China's population aged 65 or over will account for 12.1% of the total population in 2020, 14.2% in 2025, 17.2% in 2030, 24.6% in 2040 (surpassing the United States'), 27.6% in 2050, 32.9% in 2060 and 33.8% in 2100![2]

Currently, the social pooling account for urban workers has already run deficits for many years and funds from individual accounts have been used to cover the deficits. Individual accounts hence have a substantial amount of debt.

Meanwhile, the social security system for rural and urban residents now need substantial subsidies from the government and much more in the future. Therefore, the current social security system is unsustainable and social security reforms are imperative.

The Current Social Security System in China

China's social security system consists of two parts, one for urban formal sector workers and the other for rural farmers and non-working urban residents. The two systems are completely different in terms of contribution and benefits.

Social security for urban workers in formal sectors

In the early 1950s China's social security system was set up for workers of state-owned enterprises (SOEs), collectively owned enterprises (COEs), government administrative units (e.g. Ministry of Transportation) and

---

[2] United Nations, Department of Economic and Social Affairs, Population Division, 2015, *World Population Prospects: The 2015 Revision*, CD-ROM Edition.

operative units (e.g. Peking University).[3] The social security system was run by the government. During the Cultural Revolution (1966–1976), the economy was in chaos and the social security system faced severe payment crisis, and each SOE had to pay its retirees from its own revenues.[4]

In 1978, China began to reform its centrally planned economy and re-establish its social security system after economic reforms. In the early 1980s, SOEs were given the freedom to pursue profits, pay taxes to the government and compete with each other. Some unprofitable SOEs were unable to pay pension to their retirees.

In 1986, the government began to pool all the enterprises' social security accounts together and let the local government run the system.[5] Employees contributed 3% of their wages and the employers 15% of the pre-tax wages.

In June 1991, a three-tier system was established. The first tier covers basic pension for all workers financed by enterprises, employees and the state. The second tier is the supplementary pension financed by employers. The third tier is the voluntary individual pension.

In 1995, the State Council decided to establish individual pension accounts and social pooling accounts.[6] It expanded the pension system to all urban workers regardless of the ownership of enterprises. The State Council gave local governments two options, "large personal account and small social pool" or "small personal account and large social pool".

---

[3] China's pension system was established on 26 February 1951 based on the regulation of the State Council, *Labour Security Regulations of the People's Republic of China*. Only employers contributed to the social pooling account. Due to the financial situation, the pension system only covered urban workers then.

[4] China Ministry of Finance, *Suggestions on Some Issues Concerning the Financial System of State-owned Enterprises*, February 1969.

[5] The State Council, *The Temporary Regulation on Adopting Labour Contract System*, 12 July 1986.

[6] The State Council, *The Circular on Deepening Enterprise Employee Pension Insurance System Reform*, State Document, no. 6, 17 March 1995.

To avoid paying the implicit social security debt, every region chose the second option: small personal account and large social pooling account. Thus, China's social security system is largely a pay-as-you-go system.

The current social security contributions and benefits were set in 2005.[7] Since 2006, individuals have contributed 8% of their taxable wages to their individual accounts, while the employers have contributed 20% of the employee's wage to the social pooling account.

If the wage of an employee is higher than 300% of the average wage of the city or region, the contribution base is 300% of the average wage. If the wage of an employee is lower than 60% of the average wage of the city or region, the contribution base is 60% of the average wage.

The self-employed are required to contribute around 20% of their income to the social security accounts (about 12% to the social pooling account and about 8% to their personal account).

Table 1 shows the statistics of participants and current retirees in the social security programme. The ratio of urban staff and workers participating in the social security programme to total employees in the nation was 8% in 1990 and 33.05% in 2014. Against total urban employees, the ratio was 30.5% in 1990 and 65% in 2014. The higher ratio is attributed to the participation of many migrant workers in the rural social security system.

Table 2 shows social security revenues, expenditures and accumulated funds for the 1990–2014 period. Revenues and expenditures had grown quickly. The revenues increased from 17.8 billion yuan in 1990 to 2,761.99 billion yuan in 2014, while the expenditures increased from 14.9 billion yuan in 1990 to 2,332.58 billion yuan in 2014.

Revenues and expenditures include both social pooling accounts and personal accounts. The accumulated funds, which belong to individual accounts funds, increased from 9.7 billion yuan in 1990 to

---

[7] In December 2005, the State Council promulgated the *Decision on Improving the Basic Social Security System for Workers and Staffs in Enterprises*, State Document, no. 38, 3 December 2005.

Table 1: Participants in the Retirement Programme, Retirees 1990–2014 (Mil and %)

Year	Total Employees in the Nation	Urban Employees	Urban Staff and Workers in the Programme	Urban Retirees	Urban Staff and Workers in the Programme/ Urban Employees (%)	Urban Staff and Workers in the Programme/Total Employees in the Nation (%)
1990	647.49	170.41	52.007	9.653	30.52	8.03
1991	654.91	174.65	56.537	10.866	32.37	8.63
1992	661.52	178.61	77.747	16.815	43.53	11.75
1993	668.08	182.62	80.082	18.394	43.85	11.99
1994	674.55	186.53	84.941	20.794	45.54	12.59
1995	680.65	190.40	87.378	22.412	45.89	12.84
1996	689.50	199.22	87.584	23.583	43.96	12.70
1997	698.20	207.81	86.710	25.334	41.73	12.42
1998	706.37	216.16	84.758	27.273	39.21	12.00
1999	713.94	224.12	95.018	29.836	42.40	13.31
2000	720.85	231.51	104.475	31.699	45.13	14.49
2001	727.97	241.23	108.019	33.806	44.78	14.84
2002	732.80	251.59	111.288	36.078	44.23	15.19
2003	737.36	262.30	116.465	38.602	44.40	15.79
2004	742.64	272.93	122.503	41.026	44.88	16.50
2005	746.47	283.89	131.204	43.675	46.22	17.58

(Continued)

Table 1: *(Continued)*

Year	Total Employees in the Nation	Urban Employees	Urban Staff and Workers in the Programme	Urban Retirees	Urban Staff and Workers in the Programme/ Urban Employees (%)	Urban Staff and Workers in the Programme/Total Employees in the Nation (%)
2006	749.78	296.30	141.309	46.354	47.69	18.85
2007	753.21	309.53	151.832	49.537	49.05	20.16
2008	755.64	321.03	165.875	53.036	51.67	21.95
2009	758.28	333.22	177.430	58.069	53.25	23.40
2010	761.05	346.87	194.023	63.050	55.94	25.49
2011	764.20	359.14	215.650	68.262	60.05	28.22
2012	767.04	371.02	229.811	74.457	61.94	29.96
2013	769.77	382.40	241.773	80.410	63.23	31.41
2014	772.53	393.10	255.310	85.934	64.95	33.05

Note: Total participants are the sum of urban staff and workers in the social security pension programme, urban retirees, rural basic pension insurance contributors, rural retirees, minus withdrawn, transferred and died.

Source: Calculated by the author based on the Department of Population and Employment Statistics, National Bureau of Statistics; Department of Planning and Finance, Ministry of Human Resources and Social Security, *China Labour Statistical Yearbook*, Beijing, China Statistical Press, Tables 1-5 and 9-4, 2015.

Table 2: Urban Social Security Revenues, Expenditures and Accumulated Funds, 1990–2014

Year	Pension Account Revenue (100 mil yuan)	Pension Account Expenditure (100 mil yuan)	Pension Account Surplus (100 mil yuan)	Accumulated Funds (100 mil yuan)	Urban Retirees Average Pension (yuan per person per year)	Urban Staff and Workers Average Wages (yuan per person per year)	Calculated Replacement Rate
1990	178.8	149.3	29.5	97.9	1,760	2,140	0.822
1991	215.7	173.1	42.6	144.1	1,975	2,340	0.844
1992	365.8	321.9	43.9	220.6	2,300	2,711	0.848
1993	503.5	470.6	32.9	258.6	2,824	3,371	0.838
1994	707.4	661.1	46.3	304.8	3,656	4,538	0.806
1995	950.1	847.6	102.5	429.8	4,335	5,500	0.788
1996	1,171.8	1,031.9	139.9	578.6	4,923	6,210	0.793
1997	1,337.9	1,251.3	86.6	682.8	5,458	6,470	0.844
1998	1,459.0	1,511.6	−52.6	587.8	5,972	7,479	0.799
1999	1,965.1	1,924.9	40.2	733.5	6,614	8,346	0.792
2000	2,278.1	2,115.5	162.6	947.1	6,708	9,371	0.716
2001	2,489.0	2,321.3	167.7	1,054.1	6,912	10,870	0.636
2002	3,171.5	2,842.9	328.6	1,608.0	7,776	12,422	0.626
2003	3,680.0	3,122.1	557.9	2,206.5	8,088	14,040	0.576
2004	4,258.4	3,502.1	756.3	2,975.0	8,460	16,024	0.528

(Continued)

Table 2: (Continued)

Year	Pension Account Revenue (100 mil yuan)	Pension Account Expenditure (100 mil yuan)	Pension Account Surplus (100 mil yuan)	Accumulated Funds (100 mil yuan)	Urban Retirees Average Pension (yuan per person per year)	Urban Staff and Workers Average Wages (yuan per person per year)	Calculated Replacement Rate
2005	5,093.3	4,040.3	1,053.0	4,041.0	9,096	18,364	0.495
2006	6,309.7	4,896.7	1,413.0	5,488.9	10,476	21,001	0.499
2007	7,834.2	5,964.9	1,869.3	7,391.4	12,024	24,932	0.482
2008	9,740.2	7,389.6	2,350.6	9,931.0	14,016	29,229	0.480
2009	11,490.8	8,894.4	2,596.4	12,526.1	15,528	32,736	0.474
2010	13,872.9	10,755.3	3,117.6	15,787.8	17,058	37,147	0.459
2011	18,004.8	13,363.2	4,641.6	20,727.8	19,576	42,452	0.461
2012	21,830.2	16,711.5	5,118.7	26,243.5	22,444	47,593	0.472
2013	24,732.6	19,818.7	4,913.9	31,274.8	24,647	52,388	0.470
2014	27,619.9	23,325.8	4,294.1	35,644.5	27,144	57,361	0.473

Source: Department of Population and Employment Statistics, National Bureau of Statistics; Department of Planning and Finance, Ministry of Human Resources and Social Security, China Labour Statistical Yearbook, 2003–2015, Beijing, China Statistical Press, Tables 9-4 and 9-5.

3,564.45 billion yuan in 2014. Funds from personal accounts have been used to finance the deficits in the social pooling account.

Social security for government employees in administrative and operative units

Government employees include employees in administrative units, such as the Ministry of Finance, Food and Drug Administration of China, and operative units, such as public schools, universities, hospitals, theatre troupes and research institutes.

In 2014, 31.53 million people were employed by the operative units in China, of which 16.027 million worked in education and 7.039 million in health care.[8] There is no statistics on the number of employees in the administrative units (i.e. government organisations). Statistics shows that people who worked in public management, social security and social organisations in state-owned units numbered 15.851 million in 2014.[9]

The government runs the social security programme for its employees, paying the social security benefits from general government revenue. From the end of the 1990s, government administrative units and operative units began to join the social security system for urban workers.

For example, government employees enrolled in the social security system were 7.625 million in 1999, 17.72 million in 2005, 20.729 million in 2010 and 21.785 million in 2014. The revenue, expenditure and fund accumulation of the social security account were 20.042

---

[8] See <http://finance.people.com.cn/n/2014/0630/c1004-25215749.html> (accessed 30 July 2016).

[9] See Department of Population and Employment Statistics, National Bureau of Statistics; and Department of Planning and Finance, Ministry of Human Resources and Social Security, *China Labour Statistical Yearbook*, Beijing, China Statistical Press, 2015.

million yuan, 19.074 million yuan and 11.737 million yuan in 2014, respectively.[10]

On 3 January 2015, the State Council of China announced a social security reform plan for government employees, merging the social security system for urban workers and government employees. Beginning 1 October 2014, government employees should contribute 8% of their taxable wages to their individual accounts, while the administrative and operative units should contribute 20% of the employee's wage to the social pooling account.

The basic social security benefit is based on the local average wage, the index of an individual's average contributing wage, with the replacement rate increasing 1% as contribution period increases by one year. The benefit from individual account is based on personal contribution, the interest rate and the age of retirement. The policy is only applicable to government employees who are still working and not to those who have already retired. Those elderly retired communist cadres will continue to enjoy full salaries as before.[11]

Social security for rural farmers and urban non-working residents

In 2009, China established a rural social safety net, namely the rural social security system. Participation is voluntary and those who are 16 years old or older (not a student) are eligible to participate. The system is funded and participants have their own personal accounts.

Contributions come from both individuals and the government: individuals contribute a fixed amount (100, 200, 300, 400, or 500 yuan every year) into their personal account, while the local government contributes at least 30 yuan to every participant's personal account.

---

[10] See Department of Population and Employment Statistics, National Bureau of Statistics; and Department of Planning and Finance, Ministry of Human Resources and Social Security, *China Labour Statistical Yearbook*, 2015, Table 9-6.

[11] The State Council, *Decision on the Reform of the Pension Insurance System for the Staff of the Administrative and Operative Units*, State Document, no. 2, 3 January 2015.

Village committee as a collective organisation can provide subsidies to personal accounts.

Rural residents who are older than 60 years will receive pensions, which include two parts; one part is a basic pension provided by the government at 55 yuan per month, or 660 yuan a year (the central government provides 100% subsidies to the central and western regions and 50% to the eastern region). The other part is from the retiree's own personal account; the pension may be adjusted based on local economic development.[12]

In 2011, the State Council decided to implement the social security system for urban residents.[13] The system is very similar to that for rural farmers. The difference is in the choices. Urban residents can choose to contribute 100, 200, 300, 400, 500, 600, 700, 800, 900, 1,000, 1,500 or 2,000 yuan every year into their personal accounts. Local government can increase the level of choices.

The subsidies would not be less than 30 yuan and would increase as contribution increases. The basic pension is 55 yuan per month, with the flexibility given to local governments to increase pension benefits on their own.

In 2014, the State Council decided to merge the social security system for the rural and urban residents by the end of 2015.[14] With this merger, rural residents can now have 12 levels of contribution to choose from, like their urban counterparts. For those who choose to contribute 500 yuan or more, the government subsidies would not be less than 60 yuan.

In 2015, the Ministry of Manpower and Social Security and the Ministry of Finance announced that the basic pension for rural and

---

[12] The State Council, *Guidance on Carrying out the Pilot of New Rural Old-Age Social Security*, State Document, no. 32, 1 September 2009.

[13] The State Council, *Guidance on Carrying out the Pilot of Urban Residents' Old-Age Social Security*, State Document, no. 18, 7 June 2011.

[14] The State Council, *Opinions on the Establishment of a Unified Basic Old-Age Insurance System for Urban and Rural Residents*, State Document, no. 18, 21 February 2014.

urban residents would be raised from 55 yuan to 70 yuan a month. Central government subsidies to the central and western regions at 100% and to the eastern region at 50% remain unchanged.[15]

In 2014, total enrollees to the rural and urban resident social security programmes reached 501.075 million and the number of those eligible for benefits was 147.417 million. In the same year, social security revenue was 231.02 billion yuan, expenditure 157.12 billion yuan and accumulated fund 384.46 billion yuan.[16]

Since the central government allows local governments to provide more pension benefits based on their local development, local government subsidies to individual accounts and the pension benefits are substantially different across provinces.

For example, in Zibo of Shandong province in 2013, there were 12 levels of contribution and the highest was 5,000 yuan for urban residents and the highest level of government subsidy was 150 yuan.[17] In 2015, basic monthly benefit was raised from 430 yuan in 2014 to 470 yuan in Beijing, and from 235 yuan in 2014 to 245 yuan in 2015 in Tianjin.[18]

Challenges to China's Current Social Security System

The challenges faced by China's social security system include population ageing, growing debt in the social security social pooling account,

---

[15] China Ministry of Human Resources and Social Security, China Ministry of Finance, *Notice on Raising the Minimum Standards of Basic Old-Age Social Security for Urban and Rural Residents*, Ministry of Human Resources and Social Security Document, no. 5, 10 January 2015.

[16] See Department of Population and Employment Statistics, National Bureau of Statistics; Department of Planning and Finance, Ministry of Human Resources and Social Security, *China Labour Statistical Yearbook*, Beijing, China Statistical Press, Table 9-10, 2015.

[17] See <http://zibo.iqilu.com/zbyaowen/2013/1024/1714165.shtml> (accessed 20 August 2016).

[18] See <http://mt.sohu.com/20160616/n454826294.shtml> (accessed 20 August 2016).

underdeveloped rural social security system and unequal social security benefits across different systems.

Population ageing in China

In the early 1970s, the government began to promote birth control and in the early 1980s, the government began to enforce the one-child policy.[19] Since the early 1970s, population growth has declined. China's population growth rate was 2.8% in 1970, 1.2% in 1980, 1.4% in 1990, 0.76% in 2000, 0.48% in 2010 and 0.50% in 2015.

The population aged 0–14 accounted for 33.6% of total population in 1982; in 2014, it was 16.5%. Those aged 65 and older accounted for 4.9% of total population in 1982 and 10.1% in 2014. Total dependency ratio was 62.6% in 1982, of which the young dependency ratio was 54.6% while the old was 8.0%; in 2010, it was 34.2% and in 2014 it was 36.2%, of which the young dependency ratio was 22.5% and the old was 13.7%.[20]

China will face severe population ageing problems in the future. Figure 1 shows the trend of population aged 65 or older for China, India, Japan, United Kingdom, the United States and Russia. In China, the population aged 65 or older accounted for 9.6% of the total population in 2015, 12.1% in 2020, 14.2% in 2025, 17.2% in 2030, 24.6% in 2040, 27.6% in 2050 and 32.9% in 2060.

---

[19] On 8 July 1971, the State Council issued the "*Report on Birth Planning*" by the Ministry of Health and other organisations, requiring the local governments to strengthen the leadership for birth planning. On 16 July 1973, the State Council established the Leadership Group of Birth Planning, promoting "late marriage, scattered births and fewer children". On 25 September 1980, the Central Committee of the CPC issued "An Open Letter to all Communist Party Members and the Communist Youth League Members", calling for one couple to have just one child. From then on, except for the minorities in China, all families had to abide by the one-child policy. With special permission, some couples could have two children though.

[20] For more information of age composition and dependency ratio of population, see *China Statistical Yearbook*, Table 2-4, p. 35.

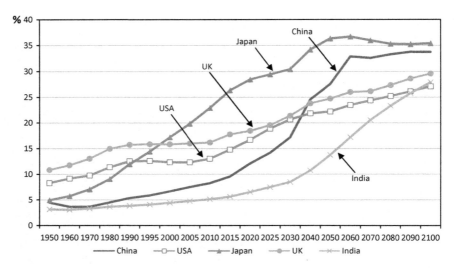

Figure 1:   The Trend of Population Aged 65 or Older for Selected Countries (1950–2100)

Sources: United Nations, Department of Economic and Social Affairs, Population Division, 2015, *World Population Prospects: The 2015 Revision.*

In the United States, the population aged 65 or older accounted for 14.8% of total population in 2015, 16.7% in 2020, 18.9% in 2025, 20.7% in 2030, 21.9% in 2040, 22.2% in 2050 and 23.5% in 2065.

In comparison, in 2040, the proportion of China's population aged 65 or older will be higher than that of the United States by 2.7 percentage points, and in 2065, the figure will hit 9.4 percentage points!

Decentralised social security system

Social security programmes are run by local governments, many of which are county-level governments. The decentralised system blocks labour mobility from one region to another since money from the social pooling account is not easily transferrable from one region to another.

Some regions, such as Beijing, allow workers to take the personal account funds with them when they leave Beijing for other regions. However, taking funds from personal account away before retirement violates the initial purpose of social security pension funds, which could only be withdrawn after retirement.

Besides, social security burdens cannot be evenly shared among different regions. Old industrial bases, such as Shanghai, Liaoning and Jilin, face a heavier social security burden, while new cities, such as Shenzhen in Guangdong province, have more young workers and less social security payment problems.

Finally, the funds in individual accounts are deposited in state-owned banks at very low interest rates, churning out very low rates of return to the social security funds.

Underdeveloped rural system and unequal benefits

Government employees enjoy much better social security benefits than urban workers. For a long time, the replacement rate for government employees were over 90%, while the replacement rate for urban workers was much lower.

According to the Ministry of Human Resources and Social Security of China (2016), the replacement for retirees in urban enterprises was 67.6% in 2010, 66% in 2013 and 67.5% in 2014.[21] The retirement benefits for employees in the urban formal sectors have increased for 12 consecutive years. The growth rate of the benefit was 10% in 2015 and 6.5% in 2016.[22]

The social security benefits for rural farmers and urban residents are much lower than those for urban workers and government employees. For rural farmers the social security benefits are minimal. As mentioned earlier, the basic benefit for farmers and urban residents is now 70 yuan per month. The benefit for urban workers and government employees is at least 10 times as much as that for farmers.

For a long time in China, farmers did not have the freedom to migrate to cities; they must work in the farms, endure excessive heavy

[21] See *China Social Insurance Development Annual Report 2014*, <http://www.zgswcn.com/2015/0630/ 642326.shtml> (accessed 4 August 2016).
[22] See China Ministry of Human Resources and Social Security, 2016, <http://www.mohrss.gov.cn/gkml/xxgk/201605/t20160505_239470.html> (accessed 13 September 2016).

labour but receive low income. The social security system is hence unfair to the farmers.

High contribution rate

China's social security contribution rate for urban workers is high. Employers contribute 20% of wages to the social pooling account and an individual contributes 8% of his or her wage to a personal account. The total contribution rate is 28% of the wage.

In 2012, the pension contribution rate was 10.4% of gross earnings in the United States, 9.8% in Switzerland, 9.9% in Canada, 16.8% in Japan, 16.7% in France, 19.6% in Germany, 22.8% in Finland, 6% in Indonesia, 9% in South Korea, 23.7% in Argentina, 24% in India, 22% in Russia, 29.8% in Chile, 31% in Brazil and 33% in Italy.[23]

Compared to industrialised countries, China's pension contribution rate is high and the opportunity to further increase the pension contribution rate is limited.

Growing debt in the social security social pooling account

Facing a shortage of fund in the social pooling account, some regions began to appropriate funds from personal accounts. Li and Lin[24] showed that the vacancy ratio of personal accounts was 34% in 2011 and the shortage of funds in personal accounts was 2.1% of gross domestic product (GDP) in 2011.

For provinces in 2011, the ratio of personal account debt to regional GDP was 7.4% in Shanghai, 5.2% in Heilongjiang and 4.3% in Liaoning. The large number of SOEs in these provinces is one of the reasons.

---

[23] See OECD, "Public Pension Contribution Rates and Revenues", in *Pensions at a Glance 2013: Retirement-income Systems in OECD and G20*, 2013.
[24] See Li C and Lin S, "China's Explicit Social Security Debt: How Large?", Peking University China Center for Public Finance, *Working paper*, no. 14, 2013.

China should not be running social security debt now as it is undergoing industrialisation and urbanisation; rural migration to cities has increased the participation of the urban pension system, registering more contributors and less beneficiaries. The social pooling account hence should not have a huge deficit. As mentioned earlier, the social security trust fund in the United States was 18% of GDP in 2011.

The new migrants contribute to the social pooling account now and they will claim their pension when they retire. A large number of contributors now also imply a large number of retirees in the future. China's pension system faces the problems of population ageing, slowdown of rural-urban migration and increase in the number of retirees.

Funds from personal accounts will have to be used to finance deficits in the social pooling account. Therefore, personal account debt will increase in the future. As the benefits for farmers and urban residents increase, the account for farmers and urban residents will have deficits and debt. Hence, China may face potential social security debt crisis in the future.

Options for China's Social Security Reforms

China's population ageing problem is more severe than that of other countries because of the one-child policy adopted in the early 1980s; the current social security system is not sustainable and reforming China's social security system becomes imperative.

Feldstein proposed that China move from the defined-benefit PAYG system to a defined-contribution funded (investment-based) system.[25] Another suggestion comes from Diamond and Barr who suggested that China adopt a notional defined-contribution PAYG system.[26]

---

[25] See Martin Feldstein, 1999, "Social Security Pension Reform in China", *China Economic Review*, vol. 10, no. 2, 1999, pp. 99–107.

[26] See Peter A Diamond and Nicholas Barr, "Social Security Reform in China: Issues and Options", *Comparative Studies*, vol. 24, 2006, pp. 33–66 and vol. 25, 99–103.

Under this system, a worker contributes a certain percentage of income to his/her personal account over time. The funds in the account accumulate according to an interest rate determined by the government and the worker receives a pension according to the accumulated funds when the worker retires.

In 2011, the social security debt-GDP ratio was about 2%.[27] Li and Lin showed that effective measures must be taken to keep the social security system sustainable, which include eliminating personal account debt by reducing the social security benefit and increasing the contribution, extending the retirement age, improving fund management, raising the contribution by rural farmers and so on.[28]

Balancing the social pooling account for urban workers

Social security account for urban workers is an independent account, implying that its revenue is just for social security spending, with occasional subsidies from the government. The account should balance by itself and be self-sustainable.

There is no reason for the social security account to be in deficit. First, China has an extremely high contribution rate, 20% of the wage income, as compared to 12.4% in the United States in 2017. Second, the worker-urban retiree ratio is high. China is in the process of industrialisation and the young from rural areas are moving to the urban areas to become urban workers and contributing to the social security social pooling account which does not provide their parents with social security benefits.

The issue with China's social security account lies with the benefit payment for urban workers which are too high in general, particularly for high-ranked workers. There is hence a need to narrow the gap of social security payment for retirees and control the growth of social

---

[27] See Li C and Lin S, "China's Explicit Social Security Debt: How Large?," Peking University China Center for Public Finance, *Working paper*, no. 14, 2013.
[28] See Li S and Lin S, "Population Aging and China's Social Security Reforms", *Journal of Policy Modeling*, vol. 38, 2016, pp. 65–95.

security payment. The government may also need to pay attention to social security tax evasion to collect more revenue.

In the United States, from the early 1980s, the government has begun to increase the social security contribution rate and lower benefits to prevent a social security payment crisis in the future. As mentioned earlier, the social security trust fund in the United States was 18% of GDP in 2012.[29]

Eliminate the debt in personal account by using state assets

The huge amount of debt in the social security personal account is a concern. China could consider using SOE assets to reduce the debt in the social pooling account. This reallocation of government assets will increase efficiency if the rate of returns to government asset is smaller than the rate of returns to the social security funds. Many studies have shown that the SOEs are inefficient.

Extend the retirement age

Increasing the retirement age can increase the social security contribution and reduce the social security benefits, and balance the social security account. The increase in life expectancy at birth makes the extension of the retirement ages inevitable. Many countries have already increased their retirement ages.

In China, the current retirement ages were set in 1978. The standard retirement age for workers (i) in SOEs is 60 for men and 50 for women, (ii) engaging in heavy physical labour is 55 for men and 45 for women, and (iii) in government organisations is 60 for men and 55 for women.[30]

---

[29] See D Nuschler and G Sidor, *Social Security: The Trust Fund*, Washington, DC, Congressional Research Service, 2013.

[30] See the State Council, *The Interim Measures on the Resettlement of the Sick and Elderly Cadres* and the State Council, *The Interim Measures on workers' Retirement and Resignation*, State Document, no. 104, 24 May 1978.

Based on the World Bank, life expectancy at birth in China has increased by 10 years, from 66 in 1978 to 76 in 2015.[31] Adjusting the retirement age becomes necessary. Recently, Yi Weimin, minister of human resources and social security stated that China's average retirement age was less than 55, one of the lowest in the world, and announced the government's intention to gradually increase the retirement ages.[32] However, detailed plans have yet to be announced.

Expand the individual account for rural farmers

The social security system for rural farmers is a defined-benefit personal saving system. Currently, the contribution rate is too low. In 2014, the rural average income was 9,892 yuan and the minimum contribution is only 100 yuan per year or 1.01% of total income. With such a small amount of contribution, farmers will not have enough fund accumulated for retirement.

Given that rural income is much higher now, higher social security contribution could be paid. Increasing the social security contribution from farmers is imperative to lighten the government's burden of subsidising the rural farmers' social security in the future.

The government could also look at establishing special taxes for basic rural social security. Currently, basic social security is financed by the general tax revenue. The level of social security should increase as per capita income increases. For sustainability, imposing special taxes to finance the basic rural social security could be considered.

Establishing a nationwide social security system

A nationwide unified system managed by the central government or its agency could be established to serve several objectives. It will first facilitate labour mobility nationwide, allowing a worker to move from one

---

[31] See World Bank, <http://data.worldbank.org/indicator/SP.DYN.LE00.IN> (accessed 2 August 2016).
[32] See <http://legal.people.com.cn/n/2015/1015/c188502-27700551.html> (accessed 5 August 2016).

region to another without worrying about the portability of his/her social security. Second, the social security system will be equalised as the regions can share their social security payment risk.

Third, the management of the social security funds can be centralised. In recent years, many Chinese provinces, such as Tianjin, Shanxi, Jilin, Heilongjiang, Shandong, Henan, Hubei, Hunan and Xinjiang, have designated the management of funds from central government subsidies to the National Council of Social Security Fund, which guarantees a higher annual rate of return than that from banks.

Fourth, a nationwide system can also reduce funds management cost and reduce corruption. Currently every region has its own social security fund and a fund management team. A unified system will reduce operational cost and reduce the misuse of the social security funds for personal gains.

Chapter 4

Financial Sector Reforms

WAN Jing*

Introduction

Reforms of the financial sector are pivotal to the transformation of China's economy. Its financial sectors are facing numerous challenges, the first of which is the high dependence on indirect financing with loans from commercial banks. Second is the various distortions, such as the accumulation of huge local government debts, crowding out of small and medium-sized enterprises (SMEs), and the rampant expansion of shadow banking, that arise from unbalanced financing channels. Efforts have been made to further liberalise and reform the country's financial system since the current government took office in 2013. Premier Li Keqiang has committed to implementing comprehensive reforms particularly to the finance industry, including the banking sector, stock market, bonds market and the exchange regime.

China's financial sector has many deficiencies. As the economy's financing depends mainly on loans from commercial banks, stock and bonds issuing plays only a marginal role. Meanwhile, local governments accumulated huge amount of debts and SMEs continue to face obstacles in obtaining finances, as shadow banking surges. Within the banking sector, the dual-track interest rate system is prevalent. On the one hand, the yield curve of the bonds market is incomplete and

---

*WAN Jing is Visiting Research Fellow in the East Asian Institute, National University of Singapore.

the transmission mechanism from the short-run interest rate to the long-run interest rate is not smooth at all, meaning the bonds market interest is not market based and cannot be used as the guiding price it is supposed to be. In addition, the capital account remains strictly restricted.

The government seemed committed to tackle the problems and various pilot programmes have been established since 2013, such as enhancing the regulation in the banking sector, stock market and bonds market; completing the interest rate liberalisation; establishing the stock connect scheme; accelerating the process of exchange rate marketisation and joining the SDRs (special drawing rights) basket. These are important steps to upgrade, restructure and further open up China's financial sector.

The chapter is organised as follows. The second section focuses on the reforms of the banking sector. The third section covers the reform of the stock market. The fourth section examines the bonds market reform. The fifth section discusses the reform on exchange rate and the final section concludes.

Reforms of the Banking Sector

The size of China's banking sector is formidable. By the end of 2015, total deposits in China's banking sector amounted to around US$34 trillion and is among the world's largest. It has over one billion customers and 2,500 banks. The banking sector has become diversified since China has taken its first step towards economic reform, shifting from a fully government-controlled, centrally planned economy into a more market-oriented one in 1978.

After almost 40 years of financial sector reform in China, this sector has evolved into a comprehensive financial intermediary system. Banks operating in China today can be classified into several categories, namely large commercial banks, policy banks, joint-stock banks, city commercial banks, rural commercial banks and rural cooperative banks, rural credit cooperatives and foreign banks. As is shown in Figure 1, large commercial banks and joint-stock commercial banks, which hold the most deposits, together took up more than three-fifths of the total, followed by city commercial banks (9.2%), policy banks (8.4%) and rural credit cooperatives (6%).

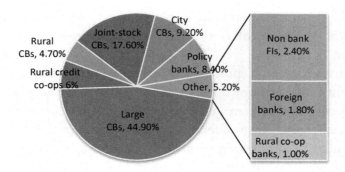

Figure 1: Share of Deposits among Different Types of Banks (2013)[1]

Source: Data from "China: The Path to Interest Rate Liberalisation", 2014 report, JP Morgan Global Liquidity.

China's largest banks dominate the financial intermediation system. These state-owned commercial banks are still heavily influenced by the government until now. As a result, under interest rate regulation without differentiating the risk level, state-owned enterprises with low productivity and risks enjoy cheap loans and big banks earn monopoly profits, while SMEs with high level of productivity and risks face credit shortage and small banks find it harder to survive. Distortions in credit allocation are thus created, along with the side effects of overcapacity and real estate bubbles, to name a few.

Such distortions have also contributed to the superfast flourishing of the shadow banking sector since 2009 given the huge need for credit that the formal banking sector cannot or is reluctant to meet. Unlike the shadow banking of other countries, the shadow banking sector in China is under much less regulation and quite opaque, thus requiring more serious analyses. Based on Financial Stability Board's (FSB) report, the growth of China's shadow banking sector is the fastest in the world, with the growth of China's "Other Financial Intermediaries" assets hitting 42% in 2012. Shadow banking is not necessarily bad as it broadens financial channels beyond the formal commercial banks and

---

[1] Abbreviations for Commercial Banks (CBs), Financial Institutes (FIs) and cooperation (Co-ops).

reduce the dependence on bank loans. The key problem with China's shadow banking sector is the lack of transparency and formal regulation.

The main kind of deposits in shadow banking is the high-yield investment products known locally as "wealth management products" (WMPs) created and managed by trust companies and marketed by commercial banks. The proliferation of China's shadow banking could be attributed to local government debt and real estate development. The involvement of local government in shadow banking is mostly through local government financing platforms (LGFPs), as they are largely prohibited by law from engaging in direct borrowing, including bank loans.

After six to seven years of development, the shadow banking sector has gained quite considerably in scale and importance in relation to China's overall financial sector, notwithstanding the lack of transparency and regulation. This can be viewed as a de facto liberalisation of bank interest rates outside of the banks' balance sheets. The interest rate prevalent in shadow banking can thus be used as a good proxy for market-based interest rate. Together with the benchmark interest rate prescribed by the People's Bank of India (PBOC), they constitute China's dual-track interest rate system. As "shadowy" deposit will not be included in the explicit deposit insurance scheme launched in May 2015, interest rate liberalisation may help rein in the size and growth of shadowy deposit. Full liberalisation of interest rates could be expected to correct the distortions caused by various shadow lending activities.

Interest rate liberalisation

On 24 October 2015, the final barrier of the upper limit of deposit rates was removed. China's central bank also claims that it will continue to improve the regulatory mechanism of interest rate liberalisation, enhance the supervision of the interest rate system and increase the transmission efficiency of monetary policy. As China's interest rate reform started in 1996, it has been over 20 years since China first announced its intention to let the market play a key role in the money market.

Obviously, domestic interest rates deregulation will create a more competitive business environment, thus promoting more efficient capital allocation. Meanwhile, such deregulation will have significant implications for the banking sector and banks of different sizes. It will also present unprecedented challenges to the regulators. When interest rate becomes market-based, competition among banks will intensify, leading to higher deposit interest rate levels, increased interest rate volatility and narrower deposit-loan interest rate spreads. Such changes reflected by compressed net interest margin will affect the whole banking sector in terms of higher costs and lower profitability.

Interest rate liberalisation will have varying impacts on different banks, depending on their asset sizes, sources of income, management capacities and business strategies. International experiences suggest that large banks with solid reputation and stable customer relationships will benefit from economies of scale and likely face limited negative impacts. Unlike large banks, small city and rural commercial banks are sensitive to funding and liquidity risks, and are thus more vulnerable to market volatilities. Their small scale and limited branch network may cost them the little market segment that they had previously secured and place them at a disadvantage when competing with large banks for market-decided retail deposits. Inevitably, they will face greater challenges than their larger counterparts from interest rate liberalisation.

A consequence of the prolonged, over 20 years of interest rate liberalisation process is the resort to regulatory arbitrage by market players, leading to the expansion of the shadow banking sector. The introduction of the purely floating interest rate will also likely rein in China's shadow banking sector. Liberalisation tends to shrink the interest gap between formal and shadowy deposit, making shadowy deposit less attractive. The removal of implicit deposit insurance and the set-up of explicit deposit insurance will further make the shadow banking sector even less attractive as no shadowy deposit will be officially insured. Therefore, the shrinkage in size of the shadowy deposit is foreseeable.

Such deregulation will unleash intense competition among banks as they would likely use high deposit rates to attract customers. When interest rate is decided completely by the market, a safety net is necessary to prevent the spread of banking sector risks which will affect the government's fiscal strength. Particularly, as growth decelerates, the number of bad loans rises. The ongoing comprehensive financial reform in China calls for the establishment of a financial safety net to protect public interest and to enable an orderly exit by failed financial institutions without triggering a systemic meltdown. The government should thus not be made liable for bailing out banks anymore. To help the banking sector and different types of banks adjust to the transition to a new mechanism, an explicit deposit insurance scheme acting as the financial safety net should be in place before the completion of interest rate liberalisation.

The introduction of a deposit insurance scheme is key to further China's interest rate liberalisation and must be set up before the full liberalisation of the interest rate. Chinese Premier Li Keqiang signed a decree (No. 660) on 31 March 2015 to introduce bank deposit insurance to protect the interests of depositors and ensure financial stability.

Reforms of the Stock Market

Beijing has established mutual stock market access between mainland China and Hong Kong in the form of the Shanghai–Hong Kong Stock Connect. The launch became controversial with the sudden and unexpected suspension and revival of the scheme, upsetting financial markets worldwide. Official response towards the delay seemed to suggest that China would not change its course in opening up its financial market. The mutual market access between the Mainland and Hong Kong is the country's first. The joint announcement on the in-principle approval of the programme was made by the Securities and Futures Commission (SFC) and China Securities Regulatory Commission (CSRC) in October 2014.

From the mid-2015 stock market crash, the Chinese government has learnt that regulation is more important than outreaching and expanding. A healthy and well-supervised environment is necessary for investors.

The Shanghai–Hong Kong stock connect

The Stock Connect scheme finally commenced official trading on 17 November 2014. The launch met with several hiccups, failing to be launched or realised on several occasions, the most recent being on 27 October 2014, which was the widely anticipated implementation date; Premier Li Keqiang had announced on 10 April 2014 that trading would commence in October 2014.[2]

This innovative landmark event was conceived many years before. The first attempt to realise it was in 2007, referred to as the "access shares in Hong Kong through train" programme. However, due to financial safety concerns and technical obstacles, the programme was suspended. The access was expected to bring mutual benefits to Hong Kong and the Mainland. The pilot scheme would strengthen Hong Kong's role as a financial centre and a unique bridge linking mainland China to the rest of the world. The pilot scheme also brings broader benefits for mainland China by improving the mechanism of its capital market; in the long run it will enhance the usage of cross-border renminbi (RMB), pave the way for RMB internationalisation and gather experiences for the opening up of its capital market.

Such new cross-border investment channel carried out through the Shanghai–Hong Kong Stock Connect will enable investors in the Mainland and Hong Kong to trade a specified range of listed stocks in each other's market. Table 1 shows that it took the Stock Connect six months to launch, from the joint announcement of the in-principle approvals by SFC and CSRC.

The connection scheme is also significant in terms of its trading volume. Table 2 shows the rankings of Shanghai Stock Exchange (SSE) and Stock Exchange of Hong Kong Limited (SEHK) in 2012 and 2013 before the mutual market access programme was launched. SEHK was

---

[2] Announced by Chinese Premier Li Keqiang in *Boao Forum for Asian* held in China, the Stock Connect programme was initially given a timetable for completion of about six months.

Table 1: Scheduled Implementation Timeline for Stock Connect

Date (2014)	Content
10 April	Joint announcement of the in-principle approval by SFC and CSRC
May	1st round of EPs and CPs[3] briefing
End of May	Return of Form of Indication of Interest by EPs and CPs
Mid-June	EPs and CPs submit application to participate in Stock Connect at initial launch
June/July	2nd round of EPs and CPs briefing
August	3rd round of EPs and CPs briefing
September	Market rehearsal and subsequent launch (launch date to be determined)
October	Formal launch (subject to SFC approval and market readiness)

Source: Compiled by author based on information from Hong Kong Exchanges and Clearing Limited.

Table 2: Top Equity Market Capitalisations at end-2013

Exchange	End-2013 (US$ billion)	End-2012 (US$ billion)
1. NYSE Euronext (US)	17,950	14,086
2. NASDAQ OMX (US)	6,085	4,582
3. Japan Exchange Group	4,534	3,681
4. London Stock Exchange Group	4,429	3,397
5. NYSE Euronext (Europe)	3,584	2,832
6. Hong Kong Exchanges	3,101	2,832
7. Shanghai Stock Exchange	2,497	2,547
8. TMX Group[4]	2,114	2,059
9. Deutsche Börse	1,936	1,486
10. SIX Swiss Exchange	1,541	1,233

Source: World Federation of Stock Exchanges.

---

[3]CPs represent HKSCC's clearing participants and EPs represent SEHK exchange participants.

[4]TMX Group operates Canada's two national stock exchanges with Toronto Stock Exchange serving the senior equity market and TSX Venture Exchange serving the public venture equity market.

the world's sixth-largest stock market by market capitalisation at US$3.1 trillion as of year-end 2013. SSE was one notch behind Hong Kong at No. 7, with market capitalisation of US$2.4 trillion as of end-2013. The two markets, when combined (US$5.5 trillion), will become the world's third largest, overtaking Japan and London markets.

The mutual market access enabled by the Stock Connect scheme is set to bring about mutual benefits to both regions in different degree. Hong Kong Chief Executive Leung Chun-ying said the launch of the Stock Connect scheme was a historical moment for both Shanghai and Hong Kong, reinforcing the position of Hong Kong as a financial centre and premier offshore hub for the RMB. Many in Hong Kong believe the Stock Connect scheme would enhance the capacity and size of the Hong Kong market, and strengthen Hong Kong's role as a financial centre and a bridge linking mainland China to the rest of the world, thus further consolidating Hong Kong's position and its future prosperity. For the Mainland, the scheme broadens the channel for offshore RMB investment and enormously increase the volume of cross-border RMB usage as overseas investors need to acquire offshore RMB before they can invest in China's domestic A-share market, hence strengthening RMB's global status.

The stock market crash and the delay in capital liberalisation

Before the stock market meltdown in mid-June 2015, Premier Li intended to further expand the Stock Connect programme and further opening-up of China's capital markets was expected, such as Shenzhen–Hong Kong Stock Connect scheme, which is mentioned in the Report on the Work of the Government (2015) delivered by Premier Li during the annual session of China's National People's Congress on 5 March 2015. However, the sudden drastic fluctuation puts the brakes on everything; the plan to further open up the capital account has been interrupted harshly, and many previous goals have been removed from the agenda. The Shenzhen–HK Stock Connect scheme has never been mentioned since then. Clearly, the crash serves as a turning point in the whole process of the financial reform, dealing a heavy blow to the confidence of the top authority; the effects of the crash will need deeper analysis.

The government's responses to drastic market fluctuations

China's stock market grabbed international headlines for more than a year, mainly for two reasons. First, the market experienced a sharp upsurge before going into a free fall within a period of a mere few months. This was unexpected given that China's stock market had remained bearish for several years till August 2014, when it became unexpectedly volatile. The volatility lasted till October 2015. It began with a bang in early August 2014, driving daily trading volume to two trillion yuan in May 2015. Within a mere nine months the stock index doubled, breaking the records of all global markets.

The crash that came thereafter was equally unpredictable. From 15 June 2015, the stock market began to show signs of weakness, plunging from over 5,100 to less than 3,500 points within 20 days, causing widespread panic in the market and significantly weakening investors' confidence. The government's reaction before and after the market crash also differed markedly from that of the previous market downturn in 2007. In 2007, before the stock index reached its peak in October 2007, the government repeatedly warned the public of the risks of investing in shares. It also issued measures to cool down the market. The recent turmoil saw the government making efforts to uphold the market and to encourage investments in shares.

In the second half of June when the market nosedived, the government went out in force to sustain the market at all costs and risks, puzzling many of the intention behind the moves. An explanation is the plan to prop up the stock market to further develop and restructure China's financial sector. A healthy and strong stock market is necessary for firms to obtain financing through initial public offering (IPO) issuing.

China's stock market remains underdeveloped, speculative and fraught with insider trading. Rebuilding the public's confidence in the stock market by creating and sustaining a bull market is thus crucial. The 2015 crash involved several new factors including the use of leverage trading and the introduction of stock index future.[5] Leverage trading includes official margin trading and those through various unofficial channels, or the "*changwaipeizi*". Top Chinese leaders were quick to recognise the harmful effects of "*changwaipeizi*" and stock index future and, from early July, passed many new regulations to rein in activities and trading in both "*changwaipeizi*" and stock index future.

The devastating stock market crash and the failed rescue mission have a substantial negative effect on the progress of the ongoing financial reform. The interventions ran counter to the more liberalisation aim. The government will have to rethink its pace and order of further financial liberalisation.

Reforms of the Bonds Market

Bonds market performance in China is much less eye-catching when compared with that of the stock market; however, this does not mean that it is any less important. On the contrary, bonds market is very crucial to China's financial system and real economic fundamentals. China has three bond markets; the most actively traded by institutional investors is the interbank market, originally set up in 1994 for lending between banks but now traded by a diverse range of investors. The market includes central and local governments bonds; policy bank notes, consisting of debt sold by state-owned banks and government-backed institutions; and short-term notes sold by companies. The other two bonds markets, namely, the exchange-traded bond market, with limited types of bonds; and the over-the-counter retail bond market,

---

[5]Leverage trading is a method of buying shares that involves borrowing a part of the sum needed from the broker executing the transaction.

which offers government bonds to individual investors, constitute a much smaller portion of China's onshore bond market.

As the roaring stock market has grabbed all the attention, the public is seemingly unaware that a big portion of China's vast capital market was quietly being opened to foreign investors at a record pace. For the first half of 2015, the central bank accelerated approvals for overseas participants in the country's debt market. The central bank has allowed a further 32 foreign institutional investors in first half of 2015 to trade in the US$6.1 trillion interbank bond market. Together with 34 approvals in all of 2014, it brings the total number of approved foreign investors to 152 as of April 2015, discounting sovereign wealth funds and central banks.

For interbank market participants, foreign investors account for around 38.6%, domestic commercial banks 52.8%, with the rest made up by domestic insurance companies. In view of the big proportion of foreign investors and the fact that the Chinese government has already removed its tight control of domestic interest rate, the interbank bond market could become more volatile in the future. Overseas fund managers now hold 713 billion yuan (US$115 billion) of domestic Chinese bonds, according to central bank data. That is more than the 601 billion yuan as of May 2015 held in onshore stocks, notwithstanding that the stock market attracted most public attention. China's acceleration of approvals is very meaningful because its currency would become more widely held abroad, which helps turning RMB into a global reserve currency. Bringing more foreign investors into its bond market could also help China's economy in a downturn, offsetting the capital outflow so as to provide some stability.

The sudden acceleration in the pace of allowing investors into the interbank bond market is indeed the central bank's attempt to offset capital outflow. The outflow of capital keeps hitting record since the second quarter of 2015. This is a clear sign that speculators are transferring money out of China and companies are becoming more cautious about holding RMB as China's economy has slowed and expectations of RMB are not so optimistic.

Opening up the interbank bond market and giving foreign investors another place to park their cash in low-risk government bonds definitely help China in its pursuit of including the yuan in the International Monetary Fund's elite basket of currencies that makes up its emergency lending reserves — the SDR basket; this became reality when RMB was included in the SDR basket at the end of 2015. With the Chinese currency RMB included in the IMF's basket of reserve currencies, foreign investors could hold US$744 billion to US$1.1 trillion of all Chinese onshore bonds in 2020, according to estimations of some foreign investment banks.

In May 2016, China's finance ministry announced that it will issue RMB3 billion (US$458 million) of bonds in London's offshore RMB market. It is viewed as a test of foreign investors' appetite for Chinese assets amid concerns about the currency's depreciation and capital outflow. RMB deposits have accumulated in offshore centres including Hong Kong, London, Singapore and Frankfurt at a significant level over the years, but the supply of offshore RMB financial assets has always lagged behind. Hence, providing foreign investors with a deep and liquid pool of high-quality RMB assets is crucial to China's goal of boosting the international use of its currency.

Reforms of the Exchange Rate Regime

China has embarked on its reform of the exchange rate regime since 1988; in 1994, China identified its currency regime as a managed float and set a 0.3% per day fluctuation limit, in both directions, for the RMB against the US dollar. On 21 July 2005, China announced a 2.1% appreciation of the RMB against the US dollar, a move towards a managed float. The 2005 announcement pledged two important alterations: first, the RMB would henceforth be managed with reference to a basket of currencies rather than being pegged to the US dollar only; and second, the exchange rate would become "more flexible", with its value based more on market supply and demand.

As of July 2008, China's central bank effectively pegged the yuan against the dollar at 6.83 to help its economy ride through the worst of the global financial crisis. Two years after the crisis, on 20 June 2010, China said it resumed its reforms of the yuan exchange rate and increased currency flexibility, effectively ditching a two-year peg to the dollar that was enacted during the crisis. Facing turbulence left by the global financial market, the Chinese monetary authority at that time adopted a prudential approach, aiming to enhance the currency's exchange rate flexibility and to maintain the country's macroeconomic and financial stability.

The year 2015 had not been easy for the PBOC as the exchange rate experienced high fluctuation. According to a report published by IMF on 26 May 2015, Chinese yuan was no longer undervalued. On 27 June 2015, the central bank said it would continue to push ahead with reforms of the exchange rate formation mechanism. On 11 August 2015, a Tuesday, daily central parity quotes reported to the China Foreign Exchange Trade System before the opening of the market were required by the central bank to be based on (i) the closing rate of the interbank foreign exchange market on the previous day; (ii) supply and demand in the market; and (iii) price movements of major currencies. On the same day the central parity rate of the yuan against the US dollar weakened sharply by 1,136 basis points to 6.2298. A day later, the IMF described the "Tuesday's policy change" as "a welcome step" that allows market forces to have a greater role in determining the exchange rate. That day, the RMB–US dollar rate declined by 1,008 basis points to 6.3306. Table 3 lists key reforms of China's foreign exchange system from 1988 until the end of 2015.

Effective 1 October 2016, the Chinese yuan was included in the IMF's SDR basket. This can be viewed as the most prominent achievement of exchange rate reforms to date as it means marketisation of RMB is no longer a purely domestic issue. Previously, the PBOC was in full charge and kept the weights of basket currencies secret all the time; with the inclusion in the SDR basket, the IMF now has the right and power to supervise the pricing of the RMB.

China has been looking forward to joining the SDR since 2009. Even today, questions have been raised as to the meaning, the significance and the impact of the inclusion. Joining the SDR has profound implications for the following reasons.

Table 3: Timeline of China's Foreign Exchange Reforms

Year	Reform Contents
1988	China sets up currency swap centres around the country to allow firms to trade in the yuan, at a rate that better reflects market demand.
1994	China sets up its first interbank currency market in Shanghai (China Foreign Exchange Trade System). The yuan's value is fixed at around 8.28 to the US dollar and the central bank intervenes to keep it stable.
1996	China allows the yuan to be fully convertible under the current account.
2001	China joins the World Trade Organisation and pledges to gradually adjust its currency regime.
July 2005	China revalues the yuan by 2.1% and revises rules governing its currency, saying that it has shifted to "a managed floating exchange rate based on market supply and demand with reference to a basket of currencies".
May 2007	China widens the yuan's daily trading band against the US dollar from 0.3% to 0.5%.
July 2009	China takes a step towards internationalising the yuan by allowing selected Chinese regions to pay for imports and exports in yuan.
June 2010	China says it is resuming its reforms of the yuan exchange rate and increasing currency flexibility, effectively ditching a two-year peg to the US dollar that was enacted during the global financial crisis.
April 2012	China widens the trading band for the yuan against the US dollar from 0.5% to 1%.
11 March 2014	The yuan's value was allowed to rise or fall by 2% from the central parity rate each trading day, from the previous limit of 1%.
11 August 2015	The PBOC said daily central parity quotes reported to China Foreign Exchange Trade System before the market opens should be based on previous day's closing rate of the interbank foreign exchange market, market's supply and demand, and price movement of major currencies. IMF welcomes the move of giving market forces a greater role in determining exchange rates.
30 November 2015	The IMF included Chinese yuan into the current SDR basket to be effective 1 October 2016.

Source: Official website of the State Administration of Foreign Exchange, <http://www.safe.gov.cn> (accessed 26 December 2016).

Since 2008, globalisation through increased trade and capital flow has weakened the existing international monetary system. IMF is increasingly aware of the drawbacks and risks of the absence of super-sovereign reserve money and the need to gradually rely less on the single international reserve money (the US dollar). Meanwhile nurturing a super-sovereign reserve money is inevitable and SDR is still the most favourable candidate despite the numerous difficulties. China has noticed these changes within IMF and does not expect to join the SDR to play a big role under the existing framework of the IMF. China has bigger plans and puts its stake on the future. Simply put, the vision of China's central bank goes beyond the ken of the current international monetary system. What China wants is an ongoing restructuring of the IMF that would bring more opportunities for SDRs to play an essential role in dealing with the underlying asymmetries. Until then, RMB as a major currency in the basket would release more of its potential and function more like international money.

IMF's endorsement would allow reformers within the Chinese government to argue that the shift towards a more international RMB is beginning to bear fruit. The exchange rate reform will hence always be compatible with IMF's criteria in the future.

Conclusion

This chapter examines China's financial reform since 2013 from four aspects — the banking sector, stock market, bonds market and exchange regime. The current Chinese financial framework is still immature and underdeveloped. China needs to upgrade and restructure its financial system from each aspect, even though the reform might be a painful process. Despite the massive undertaking, China has delivered many aspects of its plans.

Within a relatively short time from 2012 to 2015, China established its own explicit deposit insurance scheme; completed the interest rate liberalisation; strengthened the regulation of the shadow banking sector; launched the stock connect scheme; further developed its bonds market; and joined the SDR basket. These accomplishments, which were achieved with painful experiences and lessons learnt, are salient to the whole package of the financial reform.

There is hence no turning back for China's financial reform, even though the country will have to constantly adjust its pace to meet the volatility of the domestic and international environments.

Chapter 5

Tax Reforms in China:
Recent Initiatives and Concerns

QIAN Jiwei[*]

Introduction

The establishment of a sound tax system which includes the rules
and procedures of tax liability and enforcement[1] is pivotal for a
country's economic and social development. For example, the
design and implementation of the tax system may impact on the saving, investment and production decisions of individual households and
firms. In consequence, the tax system also has significant influence on
the economic growth. Recent literature testifies that the role of fiscal
capacity is also critical for both economic and social developments of a
country.[2]

This is also the case for China. First, tax revenue is the major source
of fiscal budget and the share of tax in gross domestic product (GDP)
has been increasing in recent decades. In 2015, tax revenue in China
reached over RMB12 trillion, at a 4.8% growth compared to that in
2014. In 2015, the ratio of tax revenue in fiscal revenue and GDP were

[*] QIAN Jiwei is Research Fellow at the East Asian Institute, National University of
Singapore.
[1] Joel Slemrod and Christian Gillitzer, *Tax Systems*, Cambridge, MIT Press, 2013.
[2] Timothy Besley and Torsten Persson, *Pillars of Prosperity: The Political Economics of
Development Clusters*, Princeton, Princeton University Press, 2011.

82% and 18%, respectively.[3] While the tax-to-GDP ratio in China is similar to that of other developing countries at about 17% on average,[4] it has increased significantly from 9.7% in 1996. Tax revenue funds social expenditure including education, health and social security, which accounted for over 32% of total fiscal expenditure in 2014.

While the Chinese tax system has played an important role in social and economic development, there are several significant challenges. First is the impending slowdown of tax revenue growth as a result of decreasing economic growth. Second is the fiscal incapacity of many local governments to fulfil their huge expenditure responsibility.

Third, the current tax structure may distort the allocation of resources and increase income inequality. For example, the tax rate, especially indirect tax rate, is different across industries; in particular the Value Added Tax (VAT) had not been applicable for many service sectors. This tax collection structure may distort the incentives of firms and households to save and invest. Resource is likely to be misallocated with differential tax rate implemented across industries.[5] Another example is underdevelopment of direct taxes such as the personal income tax. The role of tax in redistribution is limited. Fourth, the administrative costs of the current taxation system are very high compared to that of other countries. High rate of tax evasion and low compliance rate are very serious issues.

A number of tax reforms have been initiated in recent years. In particular, two major government guidelines define the direction of the tax reform. On 30 June 2014, a reform guideline for fiscal reform was endorsed by the Politburo of the Chinese Communist Party

---

[3] Ministry of Finance, "2015 Caizhen shouzhi zhuangkuang" (Fiscal Revenue and Expenditure in 2015), 2016, <http://gks.mof.gov.cn/zhengfuxinxi/tongjishuju/201601/t20160129_1661457.html> (accessed 17 June 2016).

[4] Roy Bahl and Richard Bird, "Tax Policy in Developing Countries: Looking Back — and Forward", *National Tax Journal*, 2008, pp. 279–301.

[5] Hsieh Chang-Tai and Peter J Klenow, "Misallocation and Manufacturing TFP in China and India", *Quarterly Journal of Economics*, vol. 124, no. 4, 2009, pp. 1403–1448.

(CCP).[6] By 2020, the government aims to achieve a comprehensive and modern tax system. The tax reform has been singled out as a major area of reform in the 13th Five-Year Plan released in March 2016.

This chapter reviews policy changes at both local and central levels in the Chinese tax system and discusses the impacts and prospects of these tax reforms. Tax reforms in three major categories, namely, tax structure, local fiscal capacity and tax administration, will be examined. The chapter first briefly provides an overview of the tax system and discusses the issues of the current tax system. Recent initiatives from the three aforementioned aspects are then reviewed, followed by a discussion on several impacts and concerns of this recent round of tax system reform.

An Overview of the Chinese Tax System

The role of the Chinese tax system has grown increasingly important in the last two decades with remarkable growth in size and the share of tax revenue in GDP. Tax revenue skyrocketed from RMB690 billion in 1996 to about RMB12.5 trillion in 2015, while tax revenue as a percentage of GDP increased from 9.7% in 1996 to 18.1% in 2015 (Figure 1).

Since the 1994 tax reform, both the State Tax Bureau and Local Tax Bureau have managed tax collection. State Tax Bureau collects shared taxes such VAT and Local Tax Bureau collects local taxes such as business tax.[7]

One salient feature of the Chinese tax system is the extremely important role of the local government. Local governments (i.e. provincial- and subprovincial-level governments) play a pivotal role in promoting economic growth and financing social expenditure

---

[6] <http://news.xinhuanet.com/politics/2014-06/30/c_1111388165.htm> (accessed 10 June 2016).

[7] Christine Wong and Richard Bird, "China's Public Finance, a Work in Progress", in Loren Brandt and Thomas Rawski (eds.), *China's Great Economic Transformation*, New York, Cambridge University Press, 2008.

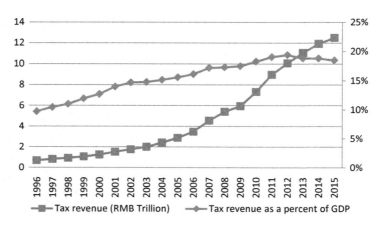

Figure 1: Tax Revenue and Its Percentage to GDP

Sources: Ministry of Finance website and *China Statistical Yearbooks*, various years.

including education and health expenditure.[8] However, local governments' fiscal capacity and expenditure responsibility could hardly match: the fiscal capacity of local governments is relatively low compared to their expenditure responsibilities. Figure 2 shows that local governments have accounted for over 70% of total government expenditure since 2001 while the tax revenue of local governments has been below 50% of total tax revenue in the same period.

Challenges prevail. First, tax revenue is expected to take a beating with the slowdown of the economy from 10% in the last two decades to 6.9% in 2015. Between 1996 and 2013, the average annual growth rate of tax revenue was about 17.7%. However, the high growth period of tax revenue has ended. Tax revenue increased by 4.8% in 2015, compared to 10% in 2013.[9]

Second, the fiscal capacity of many local governments is clearly insufficient to fulfil their expenditure responsibility, thus leading to huge local government debts. Local governments largely rely on

---

[8] Xu Chenggang, "The Fundamental Institutions of China's Reform and Development", *Journal of Economic Literature*, vol. 49, no. 4, 2011, pp. 1076–1151.
[9] Ministry of Finance, *Budget Report*, various years.

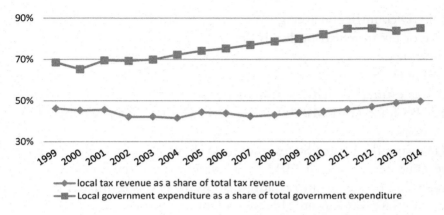

Figure 2:   Local Tax Revenue and Local Fiscal Expenditure

Source: China Statistical Yearbooks, various years.

transfers from upper-level government for revenue. Third, tax structure in China is still very different from developed countries. For a long time, China imposed business tax rather than VAT on the service sector. However, in principle, VAT should be applied to the service sector to make tax collection neutral and transparent.[10] This tax structure may distort the incentives of firms to invest and produce.

Direct taxes are employed to redistribute across different income groups. However, some direct taxes such as personal income tax are not important as a share of total tax revenue. Since the 1980s, indirect taxes contributed by enterprises including VAT and business tax have accounted for the majority of tax revenue. The share of major indirect taxes including VAT, business tax, consumption tax and so on accounted for about 48% in 2014. The share of direct taxes including personal income tax and corporate income tax expanded from 14% in 1996 to 26% in 2014.[11] However, personal income tax only accounted for about 6.2% of total tax revenue while the ratio in

---

[10] Alain Charlet and Stephane Buydens, "The OECD International VAT/GST Guidelines: Past and Future Developments", *World Journal of VAT/GST Law*, vol. 1, no. 2, 2012, pp. 175–184.

[11] Ministry of Finance, *Budget Report 2014*.

OECD countries on average was about 26% in 2013.[12] In this case, the role of tax in redistribution is limited with the underdevelopment of direct tax.

Fourth, administration cost is relatively high in China. For example, it was estimated that tax administration costs amount to RMB5 to RMB8 for every RMB100 collected in China.[13] It is extremely high compared to other countries. For example, tax administration costs in Japan and the United States amount to about 1.74% and 0.47% of tax revenue, respectively, in 2013.[14] Tax evasion rate at the firm level is also high due to inefficient tax administration. It was estimated that tax evasion rate was around 41% in a recent enterprise survey.[15]

In recent years, the Chinese government has implemented a number of reforms to address these four challenges. The direction of reforms is to build a comprehensive and modern tax system by 2020 as highlighted in the reform guideline for fiscal reform released by the CCP Politburo in 2014 and the 13th Five-Year Plan released in March 2016. The following sections discuss recent tax reforms in three aspects, namely adjusting tax structure, increasing local fiscal capacity and improving efficiency of tax administration.

Adjusting the Tax Structure

One major reform in the adjustment of the tax structure is the replacement of business tax with VAT. There are two rationales for this reform. First, on the basis of neutrality of tax policy, this reform is expected to reduce tax distortions in the service sector by providing a level playing field between the service and manufacturing sectors. Since the tax rate is different between VAT and business tax, and different across

---

[12] OECD statistics 2015.

[13] *Xinhua News Agency*, "Shuiguan gaige jie yangdi shuigai xumu", 31 October 2015, <http://news.xinhuanet.com/politics/2015-10/31/c_128378778.htm> (accessed 18 June 2016).

[14] OECD, OECD Tax Administration 2015.

[15] Rafael LaPorta and Andrei Shleifer, "Informality and Development", *Journal of Economic Perspectives*, vol. 28, no. 3, 2014, pp. 109–126.

industries, the resources are likely to have been misallocated to accommodate the differentiated tax rate. It was estimated recently that the different tax rates lead to a loss of Total Factor Productivity by 7.9% between 2000 and 2007.[16] Second, the tax burden is high for many enterprises in particular those small and micro-sized firms which are subject to business tax. From a recent survey conducted by the National Development and Research Commission, average tax rate of micro-sized firms was about 40% in 2009 and 2010 while the tax rate of large-scale firms was about 10–15%.[17] After the replacement of business tax with VAT, many micro-sized firms can enjoy tax rebate since the costs of production are tax deductible.

Since January 2012, business tax has been replaced by VAT in some industries in pilot regions such as Beijing and Shanghai.[18] These industries include logistics, postal service and telecommunication service. The reform has already been implemented nationwide since August 2013. Financial service, real estate and construction industries have been included in this pilot reform since 1 May 2016.[19] Table 1 shows the tax rate of sectors involved in the reform.

While the tax rate of VAT is higher than business tax, firms can claim tax rebate for the costs of producing goods and providing services. The overall tax burden for firms is expected to be lighter. Indeed, it was estimated by the State Administration of Taxation that the reform had cut tax by RMB328 billion between 2012 and 2015[20] and the amount of tax relief reached about RMB570 billion in 2016.[21]

---

[16]Chen Xiaoguang, "Different Effective Tax rates of VAT and Efficiency Loss: With Some Implications for 'Replacing the Business Tax with a Value Added Tax'", *Social Sciences in China*, vol. 8, 2013, pp. 67–84.

[17]China Reform, "Qiye shuifu zhedai jiangdi" (Reducing Tax Burdens for Firms) no. 386, 2016, pp. 30–37.

[18]See <http://www.chinatax.gov.cn/n810341/n810765/n812156/n812459/c1185800/content.html> (accessed 10 June 2016).

[19]See <http://www.xinhuanet.com/fortune/cjzthgjj/170.htm> (accessed 10 June 2016).

[20]See <http://news.xinhuanet.com/2017-01/12/c_1120300230.htm> (accessed 28 March 2016).

[21]See <http://news.xinhuanet.com/politics/2017lh/2017-03/07/c_129503095.htm> (accessed 28 March 2016).

Table 1:   Change of Tax Rates in Some Service Industries

Industry	Business Tax Rate (before the reform)	Value Added Tax Rate (after the reform)
Logistics industry	3%	11%
Telecommunication service	3%	6%–11%
Construction services	3%	11%
Real Estate	5%	11%
Financial and insurance	5%	6%
Consumer services	5%	6%

Source: Compiled by the author.

Another reform involves the adjustment of the rules of personal income tax. Unlike many other countries, the role of personal income tax in redistribution is limited in China. Personal income tax revenue now only accounted for 6.9% of total tax revenue in 2015.[22] Currently, tax rules for personal income tax are complicated. For instance, tax rates for income such as labour income, business income and capital income are different. This complexity gives rise to loopholes for tax evasion for people with multiple sources of income and tax compliance rate in this case is relatively low.

Future personal income tax reform is expected to adopt a more progressive structure, while the tax rate for the low- and middle-income population will be reduced. For example, the threshold for income tax was raised to RMB3,500 from RMB2,000 in September 2011,[23] which reportedly led to a decrease of 8.2% of total tax revenue of personal income tax in November 2011.[24]

---

[22] Ministry of Finance website, <http://gks.mof.gov.cn/zhengfuxinxi/tongjishuju/201601/t20160129_1661457.html> (accessed 12 June 2016).
[23] See <http://news.xinhuanet.com/legal/2011-07/27/c_121729123.htm> (accessed 10 June 2016).
[24] See <http://finance.people.cn/GB/70846/16573539.html> (accessed 10 June 2016).

For the next stage of the income reform, a single tax rate is expected to be imposed on overall labour income including wage income and other labour income. Taxpayers will be able to claim tax rebates for this overall labour income.[25] The income inequality will be addressed by having more tax rebates for some household expenditures such as housing mortgage, expenditure on education, children's schooling and elders' care.[26]

Consumption tax also came under scrutiny. Currently, some luxury goods such as cosmetic products or goods which are not environment friendly such as cars are subject to consumption tax. Consumption tax is increasingly becoming an important source of tax revenue. The share of revenue from consumption tax in total tax revenue has increased from 6% in 2001 to about 8.4% in 2015. In the State Council's work plan in 2016, consumption tax reform had been included as an important reform to achieve redistribution and increase tax revenue.[27]

According to some recent news reports,[28] for the next round of reform in consumption tax, more products such as those by industries known for producing pollution and using energy intensely have been slapped with a consumption tax.

Improving Local Fiscal Capacity

The fiscal capacity of many local governments is clearly insufficient to fulfil their expenditure responsibility. Currently, local governments largely rely on transfers from upper-level government for revenue.

---

[25] See <http://finance.sina.com.cn/money/lczx/2016-12-20/details-ifxytqav9986980.shtml> (accessed 30 March 2017).

[26] See <http://www.outlookweekly.cn/yaowen/14879.html> (accessed 28 March 2017).

[27] See <http://www.gov.cn/zhengce/content/2016-03/31/content_5060062.htm> (accessed 23 June 2016).

[28] *Jinji Cankao Bao*, "Xiaofeishui gaige kaiqi", 20 June 2016, <http://homea.people.com.cn/n1/2016/0620/c41390-28459822.html> (accessed 23 June 2016).

For example, the central government's fiscal transfers reached over RMB5.5 trillion, or about 40% of total local revenue in 2015.[29]

There are several ongoing tax reforms for improving local fiscal capacity. First, property tax is considered to be an important source of local government revenue in the future. Property taxes as a local government tax will be levied to improve local fiscal capacity. Pilot programmes had been implemented as early as in 2011 in two cities of Shanghai and Chongqing.[30]

Second, another new tax, environment tax, has been allocated as a local tax. In June 2015, a draft for an environment protection tax law has been published and in December 2016, the environment protection tax law was approved by the National People's Congress.[31] Air pollutants, water pollutants and solid waste are subject to an environment tax.

Third, some adjustments to existing taxes to improve local fiscal capacity are also being considered by the State Council, such as assigning consumption tax, currently a central tax, as a shared tax in the future,[32] or reforming the resource tax. In May 2016, the State Council announced that the coverage of the resource tax will be expanded to cover water resource and more mineral resources.[33] Relatedly, an *ad valorem* excise tax rather than a specific excise tax (i.e. unit tax) has been levied for gas and petroleum since November 2011, which implies a significant increase in tax revenue, given their continuously increasing sales. Local fiscal capacity is expected to be improved with these reforms.

---

[29] The budget report presented by the Ministry of Finance at the National People's Congress, March 2016.

[30] See <http://news.xinhuanet.com/comments/2011-12/09/c_111229912.htm> (accessed 10 June 2016).

[31] See <http://www.npc.gov.cn/npc/xinwen/2016-12/25/content_2004993.htm> (accessed 28 March 2017).

[32] *Jinji Cankao Bao*, 20 June 2016, <http://economy.gmw.cn/2016-06/21/content_20633960.htm> (accessed 23 June 2016).

[33] See <http://szs.mof.gov.cn/zhengwuxinxi/zhengcefabu/201605/t20160510_1984605.html> (accessed 23 June 2016).

Improving the Efficiency of Tax Administration

Effective tax administration is critical for boosting fiscal capacity. In the tax system, key administrative issues include tax evasion and avoidance, and administrative and compliance costs.[34] Many equate "tax administration with tax policy".[35]

China's high tax administration cost is largely attributable to the fragmented tax collection system which comes under both the State Tax Bureau and Local Tax Bureau. For many taxpayers, they are subject to different types of taxes, which include both shared taxes and local taxes. They have to pay taxes to both agencies which may tax the same taxpayer according to their own rules and standards, imposing taxes on firms or individuals. Tax administration cost is even higher when multiple tax authorities directly interact with taxpayers.

The low capacity and high cost in tax administration stem from the decentralisation of tax administration.[36] The tax collection responsibility is decentralised to county level and below (township). About 80% of employees in State Tax Bureau worked at county and township levels.[37] Only 0.1% of employees in the State Administration of Taxation work in the headquarters.[38] Local staff may not have enough professional and legal knowledge to manage tax collection. With the decentralisation, there is no economies of scale since decisions are made by hundreds of thousands of local tax collectors. Conflict in the laws and regulations is rife and oftentimes, tax collection is left to the discretion of the local staff.[39] Uncertainties hence prevail and third-party

[34] Joel Slemrod and Shlomo Yitzhaki, "Tax Avoidance, Evasion, and Administration", *Handbook of Public Economics*, vol. 3, 2002, pp. 1423–1470.

[35] Milka Casanegra, "Administering a VAT", in M Gillis, C S Shoup and G P Sicat (eds.), *Value Added Taxation in Developing Countries*, World Bank, 1990.

[36] Cui Wei, "Administrative Decentralization and Tax Compliance: A Transactional Cost Perspective", *University of Toronto Law Journal*, vol. 65, no. 3, 2015, pp. 186–238.

[37] Cui Wei, "Administrative Decentralization and Tax Compliance".

[38] OECD, OECD Tax Administration 2015.

[39] *Financial Times* (Chinese), "Mohu biaoshu Jiangling 'shuishou fading' luoxu", 2015, <http://m.ftchinese.com/story/001060963> (accessed 23 June 2016).

service for managing tax is relatively underdeveloped. Tax evasion is more likely to happen and tax administration cost is high.

Several recent initiatives have been announced by the State Council to improve efficiency. In December 2015, a plan was announced to address the fragmentation.[40] While the two tax authorities will be retained, responsibilities for these two tax agencies will be further clarified, allocating one tax type to one agency. There will be a service outlet in the other agency's service station. An updated information-sharing system for tax management, namely the Golden Tax project, is expected to be established in 2016 and all data for tax administration in particular for information of large-scale enterprises centralised by 2018. This plan also addressed the issue of international tax avoidance and evasion. China will follow the recommendations of the G20/OECD Base Erosion and Profit Shifting (BEPS) initiatives and a cross-border, cross-industry tax monitoring system will be set up by 2017.

A draft version for the amendment of the China's Tax Collection and Administration System was released in 2015 and the amendment is expected to be sent to the National People's Congress in 2017.[41] In the new amendment, sanctions for tax evasion will be specified and rules for information-sharing in addressing international tax avoidance and evasion revised.

Some Concerns of the Current Reforms

While recent tax reforms have made significant achievements, it is still too early to assess the effectiveness of the reform. However, a number of concerns have been raised. First, replacing business tax with VAT may increase tax burden of some industries, such as that of over

[40] See <http://www.chinatax.gov.cn/n810219/n810724/c1955421/content.html> (accessed 28 March 2017).
[41] The State Council, <http://www.gov.cn/zhengce/content/2017-03/20/content_5178909.htm> (accessed 28 March 2017).

2,600 enterprises out of 13,700 enterprises in Qingdao.[42] The increasing tax burden could be a result of higher tax rate under VAT compared to the business tax rate, or in the difficulty of claiming tax rebate for various reasons. For example, it was reported that some firms bought their input from other small and micro enterprises and for these enterprises, invoices usually are not provided and tax rebate is hard to claim in this case.[43]

Second, some reforms have their limitations. The progress of the property tax pilot has been very slow after five years of implementation. The tax revenue collected from property tax is relatively small. For example, the Chongqing municipal government only managed to collect RMB4 billion in property tax in 2014, or about 3.1% of total tax revenue in that year.[44] In Shanghai, collection from property tax was RMB10.5 billion in 2015, accounting for about 2.3% of total tax revenue in that year.[45] The role of resource tax is also limited for local public finance. As a shared tax, the resource tax currently accounted for only about 0.9% of total tax revenue in 2014.

Third, replacing business tax with VAT has been cited as the cause for the limited progress made in improving local fiscal capacity. VAT is a shared tax and business is a local tax. Replacing business tax with VAT is expected to weaken local fiscal capacity significantly. Improving local fiscal capacity hence becomes a more critical task with this reform.

---

[42] "Yingaozen, Chenxiao, wenti yu gaige jianyi" (Replacing Business Tax with VAT: Achievement, Issues and Policy Implications), *Jingji Yanjiu Cankao*, vol. 3, 2015, pp. 3–12.

[43] China Reform, "Qiye shuifu zhedai jiangdi" (Reducing Tax Burdens for Firms), no. 386, 2016, pp. 30–37 and <http://finance.sina.com.cn/stock/y/2016-12-28/doc-ifxyxury8953618.shtml> (accessed 28 March 2017).

[44] Chongqing 2014 Budget Report, accessible from Chongqing government website, <http://www.cq.gov.cn/publicinfo/web/views/Show!detail.action?sid=4008837> (accessed 23 June 2016).

[45] Shanghai Budget Report 2015, accessible from Shanghai government website, <http://www.shanghai.gov.cn/nw2/nw2314/nw2319/nw32905/nw32906/nw32909/u26aw46354.html> (accessed 23 June 2016).

A systemic solution to address the intergovernmental fiscal relation and to build a tax sharing system which can better match local fiscal capacity and expenditure responsibility has yet been made available.

Fourth, tax administration reform is key to many other reforms such as adjusting tax structure and improving local fiscal capacity. However, the institutional reasons for low efficiency in tax administration have not been addressed fully. While a new information-sharing platform have been planned to centralise information in the near future, how to centralise the decision-making process in tax collection, audit and management is still a concern. While there are initiatives to streamline local resource allocation for tax collection, the local fragmented structure of tax collection agencies has remained to be resolved.

Chapter 6

The Development and the Governance of China's Housing Development

ZHOU Zhihua*

Introduction

China initiated the urban housing reform in the mid-1990s when housing was transformed from welfare to commodity, and existing public housing units were sold to residents. With marketisation and privatisation implemented, state-owned enterprises were relieved of their responsibility for employees' accommodation provision, and the government's role is expected to shift from direct housing provision for urban citizens to steering the formation of partnership between the public and private sectors. A housing market has gradually developed with new rules and private actors, and market mechanism has become an important force in housing production, distribution and management.

China's housing development in the past two decades has made huge achievements. However, rapid promotion of housing marketisation and privatisation has led to controversial outcomes and many problems in the housing sector. This chapter investigates the performance of China's housing market and identifies the roots of the housing problems.

*ZHOU Zhihua is Senior Lecturer of Real Estate Economics at the Department of Architecture and the Built Environment in University of the West of England, Bristol. She was previously a Visiting Research Fellow at the East Asian Institute, National University of Singapore.

The Performance of China's Housing Market

China has witnessed a buoyant housing development nationwide since the abolition of welfare housing system in 1998. The floor area of urban residential buildings completed between 2005 and 2014 totalled 96.93 billion square metres.[1] Sales and floor area transaction of urban residential buildings in 2014 reached 6,241.09 billion yuan and 1,051.88 million square metres, respectively, up from 1,456.38 billion yuan and 495.88 million square metres in 2005, and 200.69 billion yuan and 108.27 million square metres in 1998.[2] There is no argument that housing boom has contributed to rapid economic growth, modern urban images, and improved living condition. In 2014, the real estate sector contributed 10.7% in gross domestic product (GDP), and investment in real estate development accounted for 18.9% of total fixed asset investment.[3] Housing boom has brought about physical spatial transformation in property types from a homogenous pattern in the socialist era to diverse forms, e.g. villas, gated condominiums and serviced apartments. The living floor area per capita increased from 18.7 square metres in 1998 to 32.9 square metres in 2012.[4] In the 1980s, public rental housing was the dominant housing provision, but in 2013, home ownership rate for urban households had reached 85.4%.[5] Urban residents now have more housing choices in terms of location, tenure and design, subject to their affordability and preference.

---

[1] National Bureau of Statistics of China, *China Statistical Yearbook*, Beijing, China Statistics Press, 2015.

[2] National Bureau of Statistics of China, *China Statistical Yearbook*, Beijing, China Statistics Press, 2016.

[3] National Bureau of Statistics of China, *China Statistical Yearbook*, Beijing, China Statistics Press, 2015.

[4] National Bureau of Statistics of China, *China Statistical Yearbook*, Beijing, China Statistics Press, 2013.

[5] "Survey of Chinese Household's Financial Status 2013", the Southwestern University of Finance and Economics, 2013, at <http://ghy.swufe.edu.cn/special/2013CHFS/detail.aspx?id=64769> (accessed 30 May 2016).

Table 1: Housing Affordability in Three Major Cities in 2014 (yuan)

Item/Cities	Beijing	Shanghai	Guangzhou
Total sale amount of the housing units	1,606,860	1,457,280	1,255,860
Down payment (20%), yuan	326,860	297,280	255,860
Mortgage loan, yuan	1,280,000	1,160,000	1,000,000
Monthly mortgage payment (30 years), yuan	8,132	7,370	6,353
Monthly household monthly income, yuan	7,750×2	7,575×2	5,394×2
Ratio of mortgage to household income	52.46%	48.65%	58.88%

Notes: (i) The total price of housing units is based on a unit with a construction floor area of 90 square metres;
(ii) Mortgage calculation is based on the benchmark interest rate as of 6 July 2012;
(iii) Household income is based on two employed persons per household.
Sources: National Bureau of Statistics of China, *Beijing Statistical Yearbook 2015*, *Shanghai Statistical Yearbook 2015* and *Guangzhou Statistical Yearbook* 2015, Beijing, China Statistics Press.

Many problems have emerged along with this housing boom. First, the housing market has seen a price surge in the past two decades, leading to severe affordability problem for the majority. National housing prices have maintained a strong upward trend, increasing from 2,063 yuan per square metres in 1998 to 6,793 yuan per square metres in 2015. [6] Surge in prices is particularly dramatic in some large cities. In cities like Beijing, Shanghai and Guangzhou, mortgage payment for a two-room flat of 90 square metres constitutes about half of the average household's monthly income (Table 1).

Second, limited availability of investment channels has helped boost speculation in the housing market. China's income inequality has worsened significantly whereby a small percentage of the population controls a large portion of the nation's wealth. With limited investment

---

[6]National Bureau of Statistics of China, *China Statistical Yearbook*, Beijing, China Statistics Press, 2016.

opportunities, housing speculation becomes a favourite avenue among the rich. While there is a wide range of levies and fees imposed on housing sales (e.g. stamp duty, deed tax, business tax and ownership registration fees), property ownership is subject to fewer tax impositions (except for the property tax trials implemented in Shanghai and Chongqing since 2011). Furthermore, due to low housing cost, the rich are drawn to making more property purchases, and renting out property is not deemed necessary by most of these property owners. As a result, many property units are left vacant in the market while poor households squeeze in small living spaces.

Third, limited financing channels in China's financial market, which is in its infancy, have constrained the development of the capital-intensive housing industry. Many developers, particularly the smaller ones, have difficulties obtaining bank loans, the main financing source for real estate development. Some developers have no choice but to seek capital at higher interest rates from non-traditional banking sector (e.g. the shadow banking system). For buyers, mortgage is the major funding source for housing purchase, apart from personal savings and monetary contributions from relatives and parents.[7] However, as borrowers' socio-economic status is a criterion in approval of mortgage applications, many migrants face discrimination due to their lack of local *hukou* or certain certificates. On the other hand, the Housing Provident Fund mortgage, which is expected to be a main tool to assist Chinese in housing purchase, represented only 19.2% of total mortgages as of 2015.[8]

Fourth, land supply for residential use remains beyond the reach of market force and becomes the key source of fiscal income for many local governments. As the sole supplier of urban land, local

---

[7] The one-child policy has strengthened the young generations' purchasing power because parents and parents-in-law of young couples pool capital to buy a unit for the young.

[8] Ministry of Finance of the PRC, "2015 Annual Report of Housing Provident Fund", 30 May 2016, at <http://zhs.mof.gov.cn/zhengwuxinxi/zonghexinxi/201606/t20160616_2327870.html> (accessed 30 May 2016).

governments manipulate the land price of commercial and residential uses, setting it at high prices to offset the low industrial land prices in order to yield huge land revenues while ensuring sufficient land for industrial development, which was the biggest GDP contributor in China in the past two decades. As seen in Table 2, in recent past years, only around 30% of the land area were designated for residential and commercial uses, whereas a large percentage of the land area was assigned for industrial and other uses. As a result, the market has seen surging land price for residential use (Figure 1). Local governments' land revenues represented around half of their total fiscal revenues in the past decade (Table 3).

Fifth, structural imbalances in the housing market are evident between the public and private sectors, and between the owners and rental markets. As shown in Table 4, most investment in housing development has gone into the private sector, leading to a stratified housing structure with the dominance of commercial housing and the underprovision of social housing. It is not until 2011 that the central government initiated the social housing construction plan to build 36 million housing units during the 2011–2015 period, with the aim

Table 2: Supply of Urban Construction Land Nationwide for Different Uses (hectare, %)

Year/Type of Uses	Total Area	Commercial Use	Residential Use	Industrial Use	Other Uses*
2009	361,649	7.62	22.55	39.12	30.70
2010	432,561	9.00	26.65	35.60	28.76
2011	593,285	7.19	21.31	32.25	39.25
2012	711,300	7.16	16.13	29.13	47.59
2013	750,800	8.92	18.91	28.44	43.73
2014	609,900	8.08	16.74	24.15	51.02

Note: *Land for other uses are normally offered free via administrative allocations, including land for public management and service uses, special use, transport use, hydraulic and related facility use, and so on.
Source: Ministry of Land and Resources of the PRC, China Land and Resources Almanac, 2010–2015.

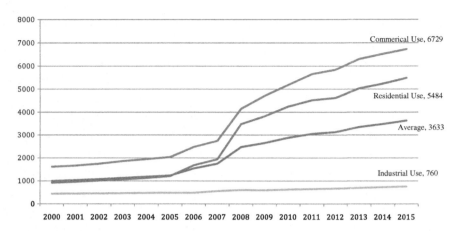

Figure 1: Prices of Ground Space Land in Major 105 Cities, 2005–2015 (yuan/m²)

Source: Ministry of Land and Resources of the PRC, "Report on Land Prices in Chinese Major Cities, the 4th Quarter 2015", 15 January 2016, at <http://www.mlr.gov.cn/sjpd/djjc/2015/201601/t20160115_1395021.htm> (accessed 30 May 2016).

Table 3: Contribution of the Land Sector to Local Governments' Fiscal Revenues (billion yuan and %)

Year	Land Revenue	Fiscal Income of Local Government	%
2004	589.4	1,189.3	49.6
2005	550.5	1,510.1	36.6
2006	767.7	1,830.4	41.9
2007	1,300.0	2,356.5	55.2
2008	960.0	2,864.5	33.5
2009	1,591.0	3,258.1	48.8
2010	2,939.4	4,061.3	72.4
2011	3,347.7	5,243.4	63.9
2012	2,888.6	6,107.7	47.3
2013	3,907.3	6,896.9	56.7

(Continued)

Table 3: (*Continued*)

Year	Land Revenue	Fiscal Income of Local Government	%
2014	4,038.6	7,586.0	53.2
2015	3,950.0	8,298.3	47.6

Source: Ministry of Finance of the PRC, "Information on the National Fiscal Revenues", at <http://www.mof.gov.cn/zhengwuxinxi/redianzhuanti/quanguocaizhengshouzhiqingkuang/> (accessed 30 May 2016).

Table 4:   Investment in Real Estate Development in China (billion yuan)

Year	Investment in Real Estate Development		
		In Residential Building	
	Total	Total	In Government Subsidised Housing
1998	361.24	208.16	27.09
1999	410.32	263.85	43.70
2000	498.40	331.20	54.24
2001	634.41	421.67	59.97
2002	779.09	522.78	58.90
2003	1,015.38	677.67	62.20
2004	1,315.83	883.70	60.64
2005	1,590.92	1,086.09	51.92
2006	1,942.30	1,363.84	69.68
2007	2,528.88	1,800.54	82.09
2008	3,120.32	2,244.09	97.09
2009	3,624.18	2,561.37	113.41
2010	4,825.94	3,402.62	106.17
2011	6,174.00	4,430.80	1,300.00
2012	7,180.40	4,937.42	879.64

(*Continued*)

Table 4: (*Continued*)

Year	Investment in Real Estate Development	In Residential Building	
	Total	Total	In Government Subsidised Housing
2013	8,601.30	5,895.10	1,036.97
2014	9,503.60	6,435.10	1,290.00

Sources: National Bureau of Statistics of China, *China Statistical Yearbook*, 1999–2014, Beijing, China Statistics Press, 1999–2014; Ministry of Housing and Urban-Rural Development of the PRC, "To Enable Chinese Households to have a Place to Live in as Early as Possible", 8 March 2015, at <http://www.mohurd.gov.cn/zxydt/201503/t20150317_220494.html> (accessed 30 May 2016).

of increasing the ratio of social housing to 20% by 2015.[9] Meanwhile, there is a structural imbalance between owners and rental markets. Many homeowners have no incentives to rent out their flats because of low rental yield. For many Chinese, house purchase is a must to get married and sink their roots. Both factors have undermined the development of the rental market.

Last but not least, there is an imbalance in housing development across Chinese cities and regions. Under the hierarchical administrative system, governments at provincial levels tend to allocate more resources to higher-tier cities and the consequent improved environment (e.g. better hospitals, education and business conditions) has implicitly attracted population inflows to these cities. The resultant increase in housing demand in these high-tier areas has sent regional housing prices soaring. While speculation and affordability have seemingly become the major housing problems in high-tier cities, many housing markets in low-tier regions, on the other hand, are hit by high

[9] The State Council of the PRC, "2011 Government Report", 15 March 2011, at <http://www.gov.cn/2011lh/content_1825233.htm> (accessed 30 May 2016).

Table 5: Key Indicators for Real Estate Sector Development by Regions, February 2016 (year-on-year growth, %)

Key Indicators	Nationwide	Eastern	Central	Western
Transaction Amount	43.6	57.7	30.4	13.8
Floor Space Sold	28.2	35.5	26.8	16.5
Real Estate Investment	3.0	3.7	4.3	−0.1

Source: National Bureau of Statistics of China, "National Real Estate Investment and Market Performance in February 2016", 12 March 2016, at <http://www.stats.gov.cn/tjsj/zxfb/201603/t20160312_1330121.html> (accessed 30 May 2016).

inventories of newly built commercial housing units, as a result of massive housing construction in the past decades. The floor area of residential buildings for sale in the market nationwide increased from 85.64 million square metres in December 2005 to 450.89 million square metres in April 2016.[10] There are also distinct regional variations in China's housing market, with considerably more active ones in coastal regions in the east than those in other parts of the country, especially the western regions (Table 5).

Why Such Problems Exist?

The role of government in economic activities is crucial for sustainable economic transition. This is particularly the case in China's one-party state system. This section analyses the roots of the housing problems from the governance perspective — i.e. to investigate how the government has cooperated with the market in restructuring a new governance form during reform.

[10] National Bureau of Statistics of China, "National Real Estate Investment and Market Performance: January–April 2016", 14 May 2016, at <http://www.stats.gov.cn/tjsj/zxfb/201605/t20160514_1356334.html> (accessed 30 May 2016); National Bureau of Statistics of China, "Market Housing in the National Market for Sale 2005–2010", 4 August 2010, at <http://www.stats.gov.cn/tjsj/zxfb/201008/t20100804_12663.html> (accessed 30 May 2016).

The role of local governments in housing development

In the planned economy, the central government organised all public resources and was responsible for the citizens' welfare nationwide. The local governments, largely as a regional agency, followed instructions from the top and submitted their incomes generated from local development or claimed deficits from the central government.

The series of reforms in the 1980s and 1990s have redefined the role of local governments in regional development. In the early 1980s, the central government delegated substantial economic and administrative power to local governments, which were responsible for their own regional development and encouraged to be self-steering in devising economic solutions. The land reform in the mid-1980s implemented the separation of land ownership and land use rights, and local governments could lease the land use rights of urban land for business uses while retaining ownership. The fiscal reform in 1994 followed, requiring local governments to share their budgetary fiscal income with the central government at a ratio according to the tax types. Local governments could nevertheless retain the extra-budgetary fiscal incomes, including those from the lease of land use rights.

These institutional adjustments had shifted the local governments' role from a follower to a player with strong economic and administrative power in regional development. In the housing sector, local governments regulate the market and are responsible for setting up market mechanisms and order. Local governments, as the exclusive land supplier for urban development, gain huge economic rewards from housing activities and have strong control over the developers, many of which have state-owned background, and were previously state-owned banks, the main financial provider in the housing market.

However, many local governments then claimed that they have been struggling in fiscal resources due to heavy burdens in health care and education, etc., which rely on subsidies from the central government. This therefore explains the poor social housing development in the 2000s, as "lack of financial resources is the most significant factor preventing urban governments from addressing the needs of the poor".[11] Local governments then actively turn to private housing developments, which enable them to keep most of the incomes from land leases to sustain their regional development. Consequently land revenues have accounted for half of the total revenues in the past decade (Table 3).

The GDP-oriented economic approach and cadre assessment system have further accelerated local government's involvement in the housing sector. Attaining GDP growth and building a modern urban skyline are key indicators of achievements of local governments and officials. A prosperous housing development could project cities an image of modernisation and urbanisation, and generate more fiscal revenues from land leases; housing activities are also closely linked to many other sectors (e.g. banking, steel, concrete, glass, furnishings, etc.) that could greatly contribute to GDP growth. As such, officials have strong incentives to sustain housing prosperity in order to boost GDP growth and fiscal incomes, and promote career advancements.

Local governments behave more like an entrepreneurial actor and regard city planning as a business operation. In the public sector, the government's role has, however, shrunk rapidly; officials blurred the concept of marketisation and privatisation during the economic transition, and their mindset of "leaving it to the market" inevitably led to the undersupply of social housing. In the private sector, the government has vested interests in its involvement as the exclusive land supplier, and actively stimulates housing marketisation and privatisation in order to derive more fiscal revenues and boost the economy. Many plots of land in good locations have been designated for private uses, while most of the social housing sites are assigned in suburban areas with inconvenient transport facilities. Most housing projects are profit-oriented, focusing on physical improvement to project an image of

---

[11] Ha Seong Kyu, "Urbanization, Low-income Housing and Urban Governance in South Korea", in *Changing Governance and Public Policy in East Asia*, ed. Mok Ka-Ho and Ray Forrest, Routledge, 2011, pp. 323–346.

modernisation but ignoring community traditions and cultural protection. The disregard of residents' concerns sometimes lead to citizens' protests against urban restructuring. In some cases, local governments, in pursuit of a sustained thriving housing development, adhere to policies that benefit them and ignore those they consider disadvantageous.

The central government's strategy in housing development

Since the launch of the economic reform in the late 1970s, China has gradually developed its own trajectory for economic development based on the experiences of its Asian neighbours and the (post)-socialist economies. It adopts the developmental state approach for economic growth which is widespread in some Asian economies, and at the same time stresses the promotion of marketisation and privatisation — commonly practised by many former socialist countries in Eastern and Central Europe — in its economic transition.

China's urban housing reform in the mid-1990s is a result of this development trajectory. The State Council fostered the housing development as the new sources of economic growth in the late 1990s. Following the abolition of welfare housing provision and privatisation of existing public housing, the central government emulated Singapore's housing model and announced in 1998 that the "economical comfortable housing" (a type of government-subsidised housing) would be the principal source of urban housing for the lower- and middle-income families (that make up to around 70% of Chinese urban citizens). However, the government changed this strategy in 2003, stating that the accommodation type for the majority of households should be private housing purchased from the market. As such, the quintessence of housing provision as a form of public goods has changed to an economic one, which also applies to the way of producing and distributing it. Housing serves more as a stimulant for economic growth, rather than its original purpose to provide people a roof overhead. "Meeting housing needs is not the primary objective (of the government), economic development is".[12]

Meanwhile, the central government's overall strategy of dealing its relations with the market in the economic transition has affected the outcome of housing reform. Though market forces have gained momentum and the traditional model of hierarchies has been relatively weakened in the past decades, the government still continues its commitment to socialism and plays a dominant role in resource allocations and market operations. It has relied heavily on administrative measures to govern the housing market. The government is strongly controlling (as it was in the socialist time), rather than enabling, facilitating and steering the housing market (as evident in many market economies). The hierarchical relations between the government and market have undermined market competitiveness and failed to expand governance capacity and build new market mechanisms for a sustainable housing development.

Such hierarchical relations could derive from the government's distrust of market power and the lingering socialism ideology, and also from efforts promulgated by groups with vested interests. In China's elite-ruled and one-party state system, members with vested interests actively develop and strengthen a favourable institutional environment for housing development. These members, though reluctant to let the market dominate, encourage capital to play a larger role to boost housing marketisation and privatisation, in which they can entrench and enhance their economic interests and rewards (e.g. GDP contribution, fiscal revenues and creation of a modern urban image for the local government, as well as wealth and power for the economic and political elites). The resultant over-marketisation of the housing sector has caused many housing problems, as discussed earlier, social fragmentation and wealth polarisation.[13]

---

[12] James Lee and Zhu Ya-peng, "Urban Governance, Neoliberalism and Housing Reform in China", *The Pacific Review*, vol. 19, no. 1, 2006, pp. 39–61.

[13] Richard Ronald and Rebecca L.H. Chiu, "Changing Housing Policy Landscapes in Asia Pacific", *International Journal of Housing Policy*, vol. 10, no. 3, 2010, pp. 223–231.

As a whole, the behaviours of local governments appear to account for most of China's housing problems. However, the central government's institutional design of local governments' role in the housing sector has enabled their involvement. The series of reforms in fiscal, land and taxation by the central government have spurred local governments' interest and involvement in housing development, implicitly encouraging them to play an entrepreneur-like role in the market. Hence, the fundamental roots of local governments' entrepreneur-like involvement in the housing sector and the resultant housing problems stem from the central government's fixation on housing as an economic engine under the developmental state approach and its marketisation strategies. In this regard, the outcomes of good housing governance is subject to the transformation of ideology from socialism to marketism and the transformation in the essence of housing from an economic engine to provision of a roof overhead. Thus, in a boarder context, political efforts are made to dismiss the group of people with vested interests and to implement economic restructuring in the fiscal, taxation and land systems, and the hierarchical model of governance, etc.

Housing Development in the Era of Economic New Normal

China's new urbanism takes root through radical housing marketisation and strong government participation, amid the tradition of social and political gradualism in its economic transition. However, with emerging housing problems and rising voices of dissent from the grassroots, the housing-led and economic-prioritised development strategy is evidently no longer sustainable.

Chinese President Xi Jinping's leadership, who came into the office in November 2012, has shown strong will to transform the development trajectory. The term "new normal" has become a catchphrase in China's governance agenda, which seeks to transform the housing-led, investment-intensive economy model to one that is based on innovation, consumption and services; to focus more on economic restructuring for a sustainable economic prosperity and social harmony; and to transform the role of local governments by simplifying administrative procedures, and let the market play a decisive rather than a rudimentary role in overall economic activities.

The recent 2016 Government Report and the 13th Five-Year Plan are in compliance with the "new normal" mindset. Both documents indicate that future housing development will target improvements to construction quality, inhabitants' living conditions and environmental sustainability. More specifically, the top leadership aims to establish a two-layer supply system, with social housing and private housing for different citizen groups, and a long-lasting mechanism with overhauls in land, finance, fiscal and taxation systems, and in the government's relationship with the market. Under the "new normal", the ethos of housing sector is changing from merely an engine of economic growth to a socio-economic concern in service for the public. The housing sector is thus expected to contribute less to the economy and local governments will receive less revenue from the housing sector.

The new housing strategies appear to have pinpointed China's housing situation. However, local governments might have different interpretations from the top leadership. They have no incentives to relocate the role of housing in the new consumption-oriented economy model. In fact, they still rely heavily on the housing sector for regional development, as is evident in high land revenues being generated in 2015 (Table 3). In addition, the regional housing policies implemented recently have largely focused on stimulating housing consumption, instead of helping rural migrants purchase and settle down in housing in the low-tier regions, as promoted by the leadership. Apparently, local governments still regard the housing industry as an engine of economic growth in their jurisdictions. Indeed, without a fundamental overhaul of China's fiscal system, local economies can easily fall back on the investment-driven and housing-led growth model. Finding out how to keep local governments in the same trajectory in housing development while sustaining the GDP growth rate of 6.5% set out in the 2016 Government Report amid the current economic downturn has become a big challenge for the leadership.

Chapter 7

Private Consumption and Economic Restructuring

CHEN Chien-Hsun*

Introduction

When the global financial crisis broke out in 2008 and global trade suffered a major setback, China's economic growth that had been largely dependent on external demand and domestic investment seemed to have run its course.[1] Economic gloom persists even after the crisis as economic recovery in Europe, the United States and Japan — China's three major export markets — has been sluggish.[2] The Chinese government has thus called for a rebalancing of the economy towards greater dependence on consumption, which is also considered the driving force behind economic growth. The "new normal" approach to economic expansion,[3] together with the

---

*CHEN Chien-Hsun is Visiting Senior Research Fellow at the East Asian Institute, National University of Singapore.
[1] John Wong, "Interpreting Li Keqiang's Strategies of Managing the Chinese Economy and Its Reform", *EAI Background Brief* No. 863, East Asian Institute, National University of Singapore, 2013.
[2] Ettore Dorrucci, Gabor Pula and Daniel Santabárbara, "China's Economic Growth and Rebalancing", *European Central Bank Occasional Paper*, no. 142, 2013.
[3] John Wong, "China's Economy 2014/15: Adjusting to the "New Normal" of Moderate Growth", *EAI Background Brief* No. 980, East Asian Institute, National

deepening of market-oriented reforms, is to ensure the sustainability of economic growth.

The three main contributors to China's gross domestic product (GDP) growth are consumption, investment and net exports. As is shown in Table 1, consumption as a share of GDP was 51.8% in 2012 and 50.0% in 2013; and investment as a share of GDP was 50.4% in 2012 and 54.4% in 2013. Interestingly, net exports as a share of GDP registered negative values in both years (–2.2% and –4.4% in 2012 and 2013, respectively). Since net exports as a share of GDP continued to decline, increasing domestic consumption could be the next engine of China's growth.

Indeed, rapid economic growth is inevitably related to the rapid structural changes in China's economic transformation. As marketisation proceeded apace, there has been a structural shift in the sectors of economic production during the 2000–2015 period. Agriculture's (primary sector) contribution in GDP declined from 15.1% in 2000 to only 9.0% in 2015, whereas the services (tertiary) sector's contribution in GDP increased from 39% in 2000 to 50.5% in 2015 (Table 2). China's economy has evidently undergone structural change as a result of reallocation of labour from the agricultural sector characterised by low average labour productivity to the industry and services sectors characterised by high productivity.

The industrial or secondary sector accounted for 45.3% of economic production in 2012, this being merely 0.7% higher than the services sector. In 2013, the services sector accounted for 46.1% of GDP, out-performing the industrial sector (43.9%) for the first time. As China's economic growth strategy shifts to consumption or domestic demand, the share of the services sector will exceed 50% in the near future. However, China's development path differs quite significantly from that of other emerging markets where the services sector has played an important role in the very early stages of development. In India, for

University of Singapore, 2014; and John Wong, "China's Economy 2014/15: Reform and Rebalancing to Sustain Growth under the "New Normal", *EAI Background Brief* No. 981, East Asian Institute, National University of Singapore, 2014.

Table 1: Contribution of Consumption, Capital and Net Exports to GDP Growth, 2000–2014

Year	Final Consumption Expenditure		Gross Capital Formation		Net Exports of Goods and Services	
	Contribution Share (%)	Contribution (percentage points)	Contribution Share (%)	Contribution (percentage points)	Contribution Share (%)	Contribution (percentage points)
2000	65.1	5.5	22.4	1.9	12.5	1.0
2001	50.2	4.2	49.9	4.1	-0.1	0.0
2002	43.9	4.0	48.5	4.4	7.6	0.7
2003	35.8	3.6	63.2	6.3	1.0	0.1
2004	39.5	4.0	54.5	5.5	6.0	0.6
2005	38.7	4.4	38.5	4.3	22.8	2.6
2006	40.4	5.1	43.6	5.5	16.0	2.1
2007	39.6	5.6	42.5	6.0	17.9	2.6
2008	44.1	4.2	46.9	4.5	9.0	0.9
2009	49.8	4.6	87.6	8.1	-37.4	-3.5
2010	43.1	4.5	52.9	5.5	4.0	0.4
2011	56.5	5.3	47.7	4.4	-4.2	-0.4
2012	51.8	4.1	50.4	3.9	-2.2	-0.2
2013	50.0	3.9	54.4	4.2	-4.4	-0.3
2014	50.2	3.7	48.5	3.6	1.3	0.1

Source: CEIC Data database.

Table 2: China's Industrial Structure by Sectors (Contribution to GDP, %), 2000–2015

Year	Gross Domestic Product	Primary Industry	Secondary Industry	Tertiary Industry
2000	100	15.1	45.9	39.0
2001	100	14.4	45.2	40.4
2002	100	13.7	44.8	41.5
2003	100	12.8	46.0	41.2
2004	100	13.4	46.2	40.4
2005	100	12.1	47.4	40.5
2006	100	11.1	47.9	41.0
2007	100	10.8	47.3	41.9
2008	100	10.7	47.4	41.9
2009	100	10.3	46.2	43.5
2010	100	10.1	46.7	43.2
2011	100	10.0	46.6	43.4
2012	100	10.1	45.3	44.6
2013	100	10.0	43.9	46.1
2014	100	9.2	42.6	48.2
2015	100	9.0	40.5	50.5

Source: CEIC Data database.

example, manufacturing industry accounted for 25.75% of GDP in 2013, and services sector dominates its economy (58.86%).[4] By contrast, China as the "workshop of the world" continues to have a strong industrial sector.

China seeks to rebalance its economy, moving towards greater services-based growth. Since the services sector is highly dependent on domestic demand,[5] it is less susceptible to global economic fluctuations.

---

[4] Quandl Data, at <www.quandl.com> (accessed 24 September 2014).

[5] Jane Haltmaier, "Challenges for the Future of Chinese Economic Growth", *International Finance Discussion Paper*, Board of Governors of the Federal Reserve System, 2013.

The global recession has accentuated the disadvantages of export-oriented growth. The most characteristic feature of China's economic growth is its relation to an extremely high investment rate. China's share of investment in GDP has increased over the past 30 years and maintained at a relatively high level. In 2013, China's investment increased to 47.05% of GDP from 46.88% in 2012, well above the world average of 22.20%.[6]

A large portion of China's remarkably high investment is however not utilised efficiently and production overcapacity is already a conundrum in China's economic transformation. Enterprises dealing with low utilisation rates have wasted their capital resources and have been urged to cut their operating costs in order to maintain profit margins. Overcapacity problems have intensified following the introduction of fiscal stimulus package in 2008, affecting sectors including the steel, solar and wind, aluminum, cement, glass, shipbuilding, chemicals and refining industries.

In a nutshell, Chinese industries have become more capital-intensive due to investment-driven economic growth. Such a strategy has therefore created fewer jobs than labour-intensive industries such as service industries. When incomes grow, the increased demand for services will further increase the demand for highly skilled labour and push up wages, which will in turn strengthen the trend towards more private or household consumption. To boost employment, the development of the services sector, bolstered by a sustained growth in consumption, is thus imperative.

Low Consumption and High Saving Rate

China's high and rising household saving rate has led to the decline in private or household consumption-to-GDP ratio over the past 30 years from an average of 46.0% in the 1990s to 36% in 2013, well below the 60% global average. On the other hand, China's economic reforms

---

[6] *Economy Watch*, at <http://www.economywatch.com/> (accessed 26 September 2014).

have led to significant changes in household consumption behaviour. Of noteworthy is the continuous increase in the household saving ratio from 30% of disposable income in 2010 to about 38% in 2012.[7]

According to a special report on China's consumption by the Australia and New Zealand Banking Group, in terms of purchasing power parity (PPP), China's households consumed US$3.3 trillion in goods and services in 2013 (equivalent to the GDP of Germany). By 2020, China's private consumption will reach 44% of GDP (in terms of PPP), equivalent to almost 70% of the private consumption of the United States in 2020.[8]

Nevertheless, several studies have indicated that the official figures for private or household consumption could have been underestimated. Wang and Woo found out and rationalised that because China's official statistics understated household disposable income by nearly 66% in 2008, private consumption could also be underestimated by 20%.[9] Based on China's retail sales growth, Barclays Capital further pointed out that the private consumption share of GDP has actually increased since 2008.[10] An estimate by Li and Xu also indicates that household consumption rebounded from 36% in 2007 to 38.5% in 2011.[11]

China's low share of private consumption to GDP can be attributed to a number of factors. First, in anticipation of more future risks,

---

[7]Liu Zheng, "Job Uncertainty and Chinese Household Savings", *FRBSF Economic Letter*, 3 February 2014, at <http://www.frbsf.org/economic-research/files/el2014-03.pdf> (accessed 25 September 2014).

[8] ANZ Research, "Special Report on China Consumption", at <http://www.roymorgan.com/findings/5593-anz-special-report-on-china-consumption-201405212338> (accessed 6 October 2014).

[9]Wang Xiaolu and Woo Wing Thye, "The Size and Distribution of Hidden Household Income in China", *Asian Economic Papers*, vol. 10, no. 1, 2011, pp. 1–26.

[10]Barclays Capital, "China: Beyond the Miracle, Part 4 — The Great Wave of Consumption Upgrading", 9 January 2012.

[11] Peter Cai, "A Closer Look at China's 'Reluctant' Consumers", at <http://www.theaustralian.com.au/business/business-spectator/a-closer-look-at-chinas-reluctant-consumers/news-story/9511aab9f882e21bad9dbf3ece23fe23> (accessed 24 September 2014).

households will decide to save more of their earnings in order to insure against uncertain future events. As the Chinese government did not provide sufficiently for social security, such as health, pension and education services, households display cautiousness in consumption behaviour, thereby leading to an increase in precautionary saving and a decrease in consumption. Hence, increased local government expenditure on health, pensions and education may reduce the need for precautionary saving and could boost household consumption.

Second, migrant workers who moved from rural agricultural sector to urban areas are often deprived of social benefits and access to public services. Hence, they have to save more of their income to protect themselves against unforeseen risks. Saving more for future needs may become a rising trend with China's urbanisation rate expected to reach 60% by 2022, up from 52.6% in 2012,[12] as more migrant workers without *hukou* (household registration) in the host provinces move into urban areas. To improve the conditions of consumption-led growth, the urbanisation strategy should be accompanied by reforms in the *hukou* system.[13]

Third, liquidity constraints in repressed financial markets have prevented households from borrowing.[14] Unable to obtain sufficient credit from banks, stated-owned banks in particular, households have to save more for future consumption. Hence, liquidity constraints have an immediate impact on households' consumption or saving behaviour.[15]

Fourth, population ageing is a probable factor contributing to increased savings as more people need to save more for old age. The

[12] "China Unveils Urbanization Plan", *The Wall Street Journal*, 16 March 2014, at <http://www.wsj.com/articles/SB10001424052702303287804579444112058812626/> (accessed 25 September 2014).

[13] Chan Kam Wing, "The Chinese Hukou System at 50", *Eurasian Geography and Economics*, vol. 51, no. 2, 2009, pp. 197–221.

[14] Deng Shengliang and Jin Xiaotong, "Excess Sensitivity of Consumption: An Empirical Analysis of Urban Residents in China", *International Journal of Emerging Markets*, vol. 3, no. 4, 2008, pp. 378–389.

[15] Riccardo Cristadoro and Daniela Marconi, "Household Savings in China", *Journal of Chinese Economic and Business Studies*, vol. 10, no. 3, 2012, pp. 275–299.

one-child policy further reinforces the need to save for health expenses and retirement. A one-child family implies that household dependency rate will be relatively low, which is correlated to a higher saving rate.

Fifth, China's high saving rate could also be attributed to the gender imbalance caused by the one-child policy. As the number of males outstrip the number of females in China today, parents have to save to increase the appeal of their son in a more competitive marriage market.[16]

Housing Wealth Effect

As China becomes a middle-income country, housing demand has increased due to rapid urbanisation. Most of the middle-class and wealthy people live in urbanised areas where housing has also become a lucrative investment. China's introduction of a fiscal stimulus package (13% of 2008 GDP) in November 2008 in response to the global financial crisis had mitigated falling GDP growth, and the subsequent monetary policy easing has led to an increase in housing prices. Nevertheless, owing to the economic slowdown, China's housing market saw an overall downturn trend in 2014. The average prices of a new home in 100 major cities have registered negative growth since May 2014 (Figure 1).

In addition, China's rapid export growth had led to considerable accumulation of foreign exchange reserves from US$3.82 trillion in 2013 to US$3.95 trillion in the first quarter of 2014,[17] thereby increasing China's monetary base. The housing price boom in Beijing, Shanghai, Shenzhen, Tianjin, Guangzhou, Chongqing and other urban areas is partly due to the pressure arising from the rapid expansion in the monetary base.

---

[16]Wei Shang-Jin and Zhang Xiaobo, "The Competitive Saving Motive: Evidence from Rising Sex Ratios and Savings Rates in China", *Journal of Political Economy*, vol. 119, no. 3, 2011, pp. 511–564.

[17]"Rapid Forex Reserves Growth Fuels Policy Fear", *EJ Insight*, 13 June 2014, at <http://www.ejinsight.com/20140613-rapid-forex-growth-fuels-policy-fears/> (accessed 9 September 2016).

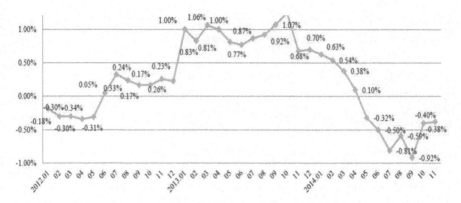

Figure 1:   Change in Housing Prices in China's 100 Cities, 2012–2014
Source: China Index Academy.

The Chinese government has tried to cool down the housing market by imposing property tax and related regulations on buyers. Due to strong housing demand in urban areas, housing prices are still rising in big cities. Housing affordability particularly in first-tier and second-tier cities such as Beijing, Shanghai, Hangzhou, Nanjing, Ningbo and Qingdao has become a highly politicised issue. Due to inequality in wealth distribution in China, the housing price boom is driven largely by the upper middle class that has enjoyed the most rapid income growth. With more people from the low-income group being excluded from the housing market, skyrocketing housing prices indeed triggered serious political concerns.

Housing prices have continued to rise, crowding out investment in the real economy. Ordinary people in China are keen on real estate investment, and some companies which do not want to invest in the real economy eventually entered the real estate industry instead. China has gradually established a market-oriented housing market system since 1998. The sharp rise in housing prices over the past decade had impacted significantly on consumption spending. As housing prices continue to rise, housing has become a major component of household wealth. Homeowners derive a sense of wealth from the increasing home prices and they therefore tend to consume more. The impact on consumption due to a change in housing wealth is called the housing wealth effect. The recent significant housing price boom in urban cities has greatly impacted on housing wealth.

According to the household survey of urban families in eight provinces conducted by the National Bureau of Statistics, housing accounted for 47.9% of total household wealth in 2002. Due to the rapid increase in housing prices, 85% of China's urban families recognise the financial value of purchasing a property. Housing accounted for 73.44% of total household wealth in 2010.[18] A national survey of 28,000 households indicated that housing constitutes about 66.1% of China's family assets in 2013.[19] As home ownership in China is high, the housing wealth effect is therefore quite significant.

In fact, rapidly increasing housing prices have significantly outstripped disposable income growth in many urban areas. Data based on 35 major Chinese cities has revealed that real housing prices increased at a rate of between 15% and 30% for the 2006–2010 period, far higher than the 10% increase for real disposable income.[20] Since housing wealth could potentially affect the economy via consumption spending, a sharp fall in housing prices could have significant chain effects on private consumption. Such a shock could lead to significant macroeconomic risks in rebalancing the economy.

China's Middle Class

Since the middle class is the dominant driving force behind domestic consumption, the size of the middle class therefore affects economic

---

[18] Yang Yaowu, Yan Jingjing and Yang Chengyu, "Housing Wealth and Consumption: New Evidence from Micro Data of China and Eurosystem", *Working Paper*, Beijing Normal University, 2014.

[19] "China Savers' Penchant for Property Magnifies Bust Danger", *Bloomberg*, 5 February 2014, at <http://www.bloomberg.com/news/articles/2014-02-04/china-savers-penchant-for-property-magnifies-bust-danger> (accessed 24 September 2014).

[20] Chen Kaiji and Wen Yi, "The Great Housing Boom in China", *Working Paper* 2014-022B, *Working Paper*, Federal Reserve Bank of St. Louis, 2015.

growth. Based on annual household income in 2012, McKinsey classified the middle class into three groups, namely the mass middle class which had a household income ranging from RMB60,000 (US$9,000) to RMB106,000 (US$16,000) and accounted for 54% of all urban households; the upper middle class, which had a household income ranging from RMB106,000 (US$16,000) to RMB229,000 (US$34,000), and accounted for 14% of all urban households; and the affluent class, which had a household income of more than RMB229,000 (US$34,000).[21]

The upper middle class accounts for 20% of China's urban private consumption. As China's urbanisation speeds up in the near future, the upper middle class will be a key driver in boosting China's consumption. Based on McKinsey's estimation, China will become a middle-income country by 2022 — i.e. 76% of the Chinese urban population and 45% of the entire population will belong to the middle class. The upper middle class will become the mainstream in terms of size and private consumption by 2022, accounting for 54% of total urban households, 71% of all middle-class households, 56% of urban private consumption and 49% of total private consumption. As a result, China's market for consumer goods will become more mature and attractive for business operations.

Broadly speaking, the upper-middle-class consumers are more educated and are therefore more likely to spend a larger proportion of their income on discretionary products and services. They have a higher level of trust in renowned brands, international brands in particular, and their consumption will lead to a significant growth in the luxury industry. They are also known to be big shoppers at home and overseas, spending on luxury goods, such as high-end bags, shoes, watches, jewellery, apparels, leather goods, accessories and cosmetics.

Based on McKinsey's 2002 estimates, in terms of spatial distribution, around 40% of the urban middle class lived in first-tier megacities

---

[21] McKinsey & Company, "Preparing for China's Middle Class Challenge", at <http://www.mckinseychina.com/preparing-for-chinas-middle-class-challenge-part-1/> (accessed 25 September 2014).

such as Beijing, Shanghai, Guangzhou and Shenzhen. By 2022, the spatial distribution in first-tier cities is projected to decrease to 16%, whereas second-, third- and fourth-tier cities are expected to account for a higher share of China's overall middle-class population. In fact, recent social and economic reforms have transformed and reshaped the industrial and commercial landscape of China's developing, second-tier cities.

As living standards and business environment improve, second-tier cities possess enormous market potential. The share of middle class in second-tier cities is forecasted to rise from 43% in 2002 to 45% by 2022. Most second-tier cities are provincial capitals, such as Chengdu in Sichuan; Dalian in Liaoning; Kunming in Yunnan; Qingdao in Shandong; Wuhan in Hubei; and Xiamen in Fujian. Likewise, the share of middle class in third-tier cities is projected to increase from 15% in 2002 to 31% by 2022.[22]

In 2002, only about 13% of the urban middle class were located in the inland provinces, but this is expected to increase to 39% by 2022. There will also be a shift in concentration of middle-class households from the coastal region to the central and western regions. China's middle class has been a powerful driver of economic growth, not only in expanding domestic consumption but also in injecting private investment. In 2012, the middle class accounted for 74% of urban China's private consumption and 58% of private consumption. According to McKinsey's prediction, China's middle class consumption is expected to account for 24% of GDP by 2022.

Increasing Share of Labour Income in GDP to Boost Consumption

Wages in China are suppressed due to an imperfect labour market that imposes barriers to labour mobility and accrues benefits gained from

---

[22] "Explosive Growth In High-Earner Demographic Projected For Coming Decade", *Jing Daily*, 13 June 2013, at <https://jingdaily.com/mckinsey-chinas-upper-middle-class-to-drive-global-luxury-consumption/> (accessed 6 October 2014).

the rapid economic growth to capital returns of state-owned enterprises (SOEs) and foreign-invested enterprises.[23] Consequently, the share of labour income in GDP registered the most pronounced decline,[24] from about 50% of GDP in 1998 to only 40% in 2007.[25] The decline in the share of labour income in GDP has coincided with the decline in private consumption. Indeed, China's rapid GDP growth has not been successful in terms of creating more jobs, thereby further depressing household income.

Since consumption is theoretically a function of income, the best way to increase consumption is to boost the share of labour income in GDP. Labour income is also the main component of household income, which in turn contributes to a growing share of consumption in GDP. In general, factors such as technological progress, globalisation, increased monopoly or monopsony power, and ineffective worker protection do have an effect on the labour share.[26] As for China, the industrial structural change from agricultural sector to non-agricultural sectors, ownership restructuring of SOEs, privatisation, technical progress, the increase in monopoly power, international trade and the entry of foreign direct investment are the key factors behind the decrease in labour share.[27]

In reality, average annual wage in China increased from RMB5,348 in 1995 to RMB28,898 in 2008, reflecting an average growth rate of

[23]Jahangir Aziz and Cui Li, "Explaining China's Low Consumption: The Neglected Role of Household Income", *IMF Working Paper* WP/07/181, 2007.
[24]Qi Li and Penelope B. Prime, "Market Reforms and Consumption Puzzles in China", *China Economic Review*, vol. 20, no. 3, 2009, pp. 388–401.
[25]Fariha Kamal, Mary E. Lovely and Devashish Mitra, "Trade Liberalization and Labor Shares in China", *Discussion Paper* CES 14-24, U.S. Census Bureau, Center for Economic Studies, 2014.
[26]"Monopsony Exploitation", *Economic Help*, 6 January 2012, at <http://www.economicshelp.org/blog/4840/labour-markets/monopsony-exploitation> (accessed 24 September 2014).
[27] Zhou Minghai, Xiao Wen and Yao Xianguo, "Unbalanced Economic Growth and Uneven National Income Distribution: Evidence from China", *Working Paper*, Institute of Research on Labor and Employment, University of California, Los Angeles, 2014.

14.2%.[28] During the 12th Five-Year Programme (2011–2015) period, wage rate increased by more than 13% per year.[29] An important driver behind the wage growth is the gradual increase in the minimum wage. As of 1 June 2014, the city with the highest monthly minimum wage was Shanghai (RMB1,820), followed by Shenzhen (RMB1,808). Guizhou had the lowest minimum wage at RMB1,030.[30] The highest minimum wages are in the coastal provinces and the lowest wages are in the central and western provinces.

Given the challenges, it is unlikely that China will adhere to an investment-driven growth due to its increasingly inefficient investments and tighter financing constraints. A greater dependence on the market mechanism to increase capital efficiency and productivity is inevitable. As China looks ahead, ensuring robust consumption will be the solution to a sustainable growth. Increasing the labour income share in GDP and promoting domestic consumption will hence yield decisive results in rebalancing China's economy.

---

[28] "Paradise Reconsidered", *China Economic Review*, 1 May 2011, at <http://www.chinaeconomicreview.com/content/paradise-reconsidered> (accessed 28 September 2014).

[29] KPMG, "China's 12th Five-Year Plan: Consumer Market", at <http://www.kpmg.com/> (accessed 24 September 2014).

[30] *China Labour Bulletin*, at < http://www.clb.org.hk/> (accessed 24 September 2014).

Chapter 8

Agriculture: Circulation and Management of Grain Reserves

Jane DU*

Introduction

China's laborious effort to maintain food security to feed its massive population has long been well known. Food security has received renewed attention since 2008 with the promulgation of the Medium- and Long-term Plan for National Food Security 2008–2020. In the pursuit of grain works, achieving the strategic grain reserve is chosen as the major policy instrument to prevent output shortfalls and to fulfil China's food security policy goal.

China's food security has evolved over time with respect to its goals. Overall, its post-1978 grain policies may be divided into roughly four phases: 1979–1984; 1985–1992; 1993–2002; and 2003 to the present. During the 1979–1984 period, when grain production quickly recovered as a result of a sharp increase in procurement price, the lack of fiscal capacity became a challenge. After a new price control policy was introduced in 1984, post-1985 slowdown in grain output set in. To escape years of grain supply instability, the state raised grain purchase price during the second phase (1985–1992). Towards the end of the

---

* Jane DU is Visiting Research Fellow at the East Asian Institute, National University of Singapore.

1980s, as bumper harvests again severely affected central finance, the government started to reduce urban grain subsidies. During the third phase (1993–2002), new efforts were made to centralise grain management and government monopoly to counter soaring prices. The Grain Bureau was entrusted with most grain pricing rights, which seriously depressed the farmgate grain purchasing price. In 2003, China experienced the largest grain supply crisis since 1979, thus forcing the government to fully open up its grain market until today.

China's food security has two major concerns — food availability and food accessibility. In recent years, China's per capita grain possession remains at a historical high, indicating China's self-sufficiency and consistency in food supply. However, food accessibility witnessed a different trend. After 2003, China's consumer price index (CPI) entered into a monotonically increasing path and accelerated from 2008 onwards. Grain retail price increased correspondingly, weakening food accessibility for consumption. This development had attracted renewed attention from the Chinese government to food security and aroused considerable interest in rebuilding grain reserve.

In the current phase, the Chinese government has re-emphasised the need to enhance food accessibility by rebuilding grain reserve to address physical interruptions in grain supplies in order to stabilise selling price in grain market. This requires not only substantial central financial support but also an efficient storage mechanism. The grain sector in China is now largely market-oriented, depending solely on grain reserve to ensure food security. Challenges abound, such as cost of establishing and maintaining the grain reserve; grain price fluctuations due to influence from the international market; and inequality in domestic grain accessibility for low-income households in China.

Post-1979 Reforms of the Grain Circulation System

After the Great Famine and the Cultural Revolution (*wenhua da geming*), China prioritised grain production at the beginning of the post-1979 reform. The first phase of reform was carried out through decollectivisation via the introduction of home responsibility system. Alongside the implementation of home responsibility system and a sharp rise in grain purchase price, 1984 saw successive harvests.[1] However, with rapid growth in grain output and substantial increase in grain pricing, another problem began to emerge — the state's fiscal problem. There are various ways to ease fiscal pressure. The most direct measure is to reduce the quantity of grain purchases or lower the grain purchase price. Since the former measure may pose immediate threat to food supply, the central turned to the latter. In 1985, the "reverse 30:70 ratio" (*dao san qi*) was introduced.[2] On the surface, this new rule appeared to offer farmers an even higher quota price. However, in reality, it did not generate higher marginal income since the "above-quota price" under the "reverse 30:70 ration" pricing rule was lowered to the level of the preceding year's quota price. As a result of the rapid changes to the grain purchase price during the recovery period, the post-1985 slowdown in grain production set in (Figure 1).

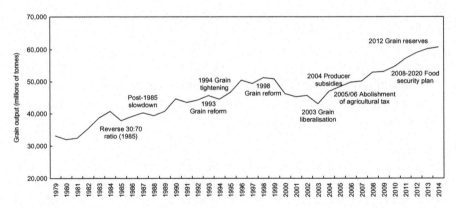

Figure 1:   Total Grain Output and the Evolution of Major Grain Policies in China, 1979–2014

Source: National Bureau of Statistics of China, *China Statistical Yearbook*, various editions, Beijing, China Statistics Press, various years.

---

[1] The real grain purchase price increase is calculated from the grain price and consumer price index (CPI) from *China Statistical Yearbooks*. Compared with that of 1978, the real rice price rose by 36.79% in 1984 alone (64.02% in nominal terms).

[2] Under this policy, the new contractual grain purchase price consisted of 30% of purchases being made at the stipulated quota price and 70% at above the quota price.

In order to guarantee food supply, the Chinese government introduced a set of price incentive policies towards the end of the 1980s. Grain output subsequently started to recover from the post-1985 slowdown. In 1990, China's grain production reached its second historical peak.[3] This required a large fiscal budget for the state to purchase and circulate grain. The continuous fiscal pressure compelled the government to "open grain pricing and marketing in the next two to three years (to the market)".[4]

However, high inflation in the early 1990s raised the urban grain selling price sharply in the 1993–1994 period.[5] To maintain social stability, the state took back its control rights over all grain works from the market in 1994, rescinding the marketisation of grain circulation. To stabilise grain supply, the state increased grain purchase price in 1995–1996. As a result, grain output in 1995–1997 period soared to the highest level recorded in China's history.[6] However, the increase in the grain purchase price, together with a strengthened grain circulation system, brought about not only bumper harvests but also an unprecedentedly large fiscal deficit to the state. In 1998, the central government in its Document No. 15 published in 1998 explicitly stated that "the central government's finance was now overwhelmed".[7]

Accordingly, the 1998 grain reform started, requiring grain bureaus to practise their own independent accounting. Although the 1998

---

[3] The 1990 grain output was 446.24 million tonnes, 9.56% higher than the first peak level (1984) in history and nearly 46.42% higher than that in 1978.

[4] State Council Document No. 9 (1993), *Circular of the State Council on Speeding up Reform of the Grain Circulation System*, Beijing, The State Council, 15 February 1993.

[5] The 1993 and 1994 CPI, compared to that of the preceding year, increased by 14.70% and 24.13%, respectively.

[6] In 1995, rice and wheat output levels were in line with those of 1990. The 1996 output increased slightly. In 1997, both rice and wheat outputs reached the highest level since 1949, with rice output hitting 200.73 million tonnes (6.02% higher than the next highest record in 1990) and wheat output attaining 123.29 million tonnes (25.51% higher than that of 1990).

[7] State Council Document No. 15 (1998), *Decision of the State Council on Further Reform over the Grain Circulation System* (Beijing: The State Council, 10 May 1998).

reform eventually achieved fiscal alleviation, all grain pricing rights were relinquished to the state-owned grain enterprises. The 1998 Grain Purchase Regulations also prescribed state-owned grain enterprises' remit in trading and limits, beyond which they were not allowed to operate. At the end of the 1998 grain reform, the central government had successfully avoided a grain deficit. In fact the 1998 grain reform provided an opportunity for local grain bureaus to depress farmgate purchase price in order to make profit. Together with a further decrease in the real purchase price, the output of rice and wheat had dropped consecutively. In 2003, the output of rice and wheat reached the 1982 and 1984 levels, respectively.[8] The Chinese government apparently experienced the largest systemic grain crisis since the end of the Cultural Revolution.

The 2003 crisis eventually forced the Chinese government to open up the grain market fully and rebuild the state subsidy mechanism (for producers).[9] In the subsequent Document No. 17 issued in 2004,[10] the government adjusted the protected prices for major grain crops in the main producing provinces and county-level governments started to grant direct subsidies to grain-planting households. After 2004, China reverted to a market-oriented grain policy. In government Document No. 1s published in 2005 and 2006, the state gradually phased out agricultural tax. In subsequent years as reflected in the Document No. 1s in 2007 and 2008, the state increased the subsidies for grain production and further endorsed marketisation as the main approach in China's agricultural reform.

---

[8] The 2003 rice and wheat output was 80.03% and 70.15% that of 1997 prices, respectively.

[9] Central Committee Document No. 1 (2004), *Opinions of the Central Committee of the CCP and the State Council Concerning Several Policies on Promoting the Increase of Farmers' Income*, Beijing, Communist Party of China, Central Committee and State Council, 31 December 2003.

[10] State Council Document No. 17 (2004), *Opinions of the State Council on Further Deepening the Reform to the Grain Distribution System*, Beijing, The State Council, 23 May 2004.

China's Food Security: Availability vs. Accessibility

At the end of 2008, as stipulated in the Medium- and Long-term Plan for National Food Security (2008–2020), the state re-emphasised China's food security. Unlike reforms in previous years, grain production from 2008 to 2014 remained at historic highs (Figure 1). From food self-sufficiency perspective, years of grain harvests ensured national food security. However China has, since 2008, undergone another round of high inflation. Unlike the 1988–1992 period, an increase in the grain production cost could be compensated by a rise in the nominal grain selling price as decided by the market. However this would, in return, weaken China's food accessibility.

From 2012 to 2014, the Chinese government re-emphasised food accessibility by focusing on the grain reserve. In principle, grain reserve is used primarily to address physical interruptions in grain supplies so as to stabilise grain market selling price and guard against any outbreak of a national grain crisis. However, maintaining a large-scale and more efficiently managed grain reserve requires a more "efficient" storage mechanism and adequate central financial support. This was made possible after more than three decades of economic growth. When food security problems highlight the urgent need for grain reserve operations, the state's future policy should concentrate less on changing the basic principles underlying China's grain reserve strategy, but more on enhancing the efficiency of the existing system.

To provide a sound evaluation of China's food accessibility, the development of China's food supply in recent decades have to be examined. As is shown in Table 1, output of the three major crops — rice, wheat and corn — has grown steadily and significantly since the 1950s. In 2014, the production of the three major grain crops reached their historical peak. Even taking China's population growth into consideration, per capita grain possession is shown to have increased considerably (Table 1). This indicates that China's per capita grain availability based on domestic production, excluding imports, has achieved a historical high in recent years. As such, the Chinese government's heightened food security concern in 2008 is apparently out of fear of inadequate grain production.

Table 1:   China's Grain Output and Per Capita Grain Possession, 1949–2014

Year	Rice (million tonnes)	Wheat (million tonnes)	Corn (million tonnes)	Per Capita Grain Possession (kilogrammes per person)
1949	48.65	13.82	12.42	208.95
1958	80.85	22.59	23.13	299.52
1966	95.39	25.28	28.43	287.10
1979	143.75	62.73	60.04	340.48
1984	178.26	87.82	73.41	390.30
1990	189.33	98.23	96.82	390.30
1998	198.71	109.73	132.95	410.62
2014	206.51	126.21	215.65	443.79

Source: National Bureau of Statistics of China, China Statistical Yearbook, various editions, Beijing, Chinese Statistics Press, various years.

When fear of production shortfall or a lack of grain availability fails to lend a plausible rationale behind the Chinese government's concerns for food security, a possible factor is grain accessibility, or simply, the grain price. Indeed, China had encountered three major rounds of high inflation since the end of 1978, notably, the 1985 to 1989 period, the 1993 to 1998 period and the post-2008 period (Figure 2). China's inflation in fact started in 2003 when CPI entered a monotonically increasing path and then accelerated from 2008 (Figure 2). Alongside the overall CPI changes, grain price movement demonstrated a similar pattern (Figure 3, Panel (a)). More specifically, grain retail price rebounded and, in 2008, reached the third historical high in real terms (Figure 3, Panel (b)).

An understanding of the importance of grain reserves to the Chinese government would shed light on the changes in grain prices, especially the gradual but consistent rise in prices since 2008.[11] Unlike the price

---

[11] China's concern over food security started in 2008, as reflected in the Medium- and Long-term Plan for National Food Security 2008–2010, the National Development and Reform Commission, 2008.

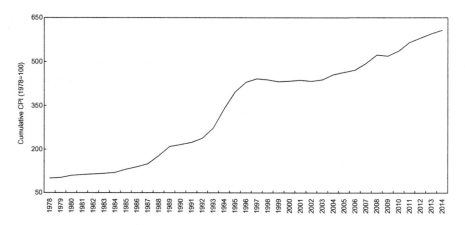

Figure 2: Cumulative CPI in China, 1978–2014

Source: National Bureau of Statistics of China, *China Statistical Yearbook*, various editions, Beijing, China Statistics Press, various years.

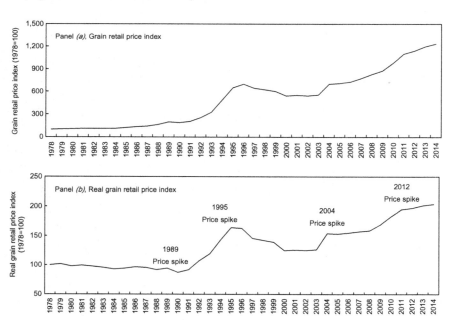

Figure 3: China's Grain Retail Price and Real Grain Retail Price Indices, 1978–2014

Source: National Bureau of Statistics of China, *China Statistical Yearbook*, various editions, Beijing, China Statistics Press, various years.

hikes of 1989 and 1995, the 2004 and 2012 price spikes occurred largely as a response to the grain market liberation that started in 2003. For most of the post-1949, maintaining a low grain selling price was regarded as equivalent to strengthened food accessibility in China. This would be true as long as the state monopolises the grain circulation system and that the state could obtain sufficient surplus from grain production. However, this had changed in 2003 when China's grain circulation system was opened to non-state sectors and achieved basic liberalisation. As a result, the state can no longer use price control to ensure grain accessibility to consumers. As an alternative, the government turned to grain reserve as an effective tool to intervene in the market and to stabilise grain prices.

In addition to the government's market intervention by assuming the management of grain reserve, increasing household disposal income also ensures food accessibility. Indeed, as income grows, the share of household expenditure on grains and other basic food stuff will decline. As a result, grain price hikes will not significantly affect the standard of living of households. As is shown in Table 2, between 1981 and 2012, per capita disposable income for urban households

Table 2: Urban Households' Per Capita Disposable Income and Grain Expenditures

	1981	1993	1998	2003	2008	2012
Urban households' per capita disposable income (yuan)	500	2,577	5,425	8,472	15,781	26,959
Urban households' per capita expenditure on grain consumption (yuan)	59	130	227	194	328	459
Share of grain expenditure in urban households' per capita income (%)	11.8%	5.0%	4.2%	2.3%	2.1%	1.7%

Source: National Bureau of Statistics of China, *China Statistical Yearbook*, various editions, Beijing, China Statistics Press, various years.

increased by 53 times in nominal terms, while the share of grain expenditure in urban household per capita income declined from 11.8% in 1981 to less than 1.7% in 2012. As such, expenditure on grain consumption would unlikely drive Chinese household finance into a corner.

Therefore, as discussed, anxieties about production shortage and deteriorating access to food are not the underlying factors for the Chinese government's renewed concern over food security. On the one hand, grain production has been increasing in recent years to reach historical highs. On the other hand, despite rising grain prices, dispensable household income has risen at a faster rate to ensure food accessibility. The question then remains as to what aspects China considers most important in food security.

Food Security Achieved by State Intervention

China's food security goes beyond securing food supply and is instead a national security issue. Indeed, for most of the years after 1949, food security has been a top priority for the central government. This is reflected in the secrecy surrounding food security, such as the amount of grain assigned either for circulation or for reserve, as well as the opaque nature of the institutions responsible for making and implementing grain policies. Underlying the secrecy is the state's strong desire to control all grain-related issues, including production and pricing. The Chinese government had monopolised the grain sector for 50 years. Through the years right up until 2003 when the grain market was liberalised, China's food security was achieved through a closed system monopolised by the state. The state used compulsory procurement to guarantee grain supply, and accessibility was ensured through urban grain subsidies and grain reserve.

Under such a system of state monopoly, relevant costs were financed by the government. Over time, this proved to be a growing fiscal burden to the government when grain price rose and production increased. This arrangement, however, often led to conflicting outcomes for the central government. For example, to ensure food availability, the state might increase procurement price to stimulate production. However, pushing for higher production required higher fiscal expenditure by the government, including higher grain purchase fund, higher administrative cost in grain circulation and more urban grain subsidies. As such, fiscal expenditure increases when food availability is enhanced.

Under state monopoly, the state's fiscal balance was positive. At times when the central government experienced financial difficulties, the state might have to resort to measures, such as lowering grain purchase price or raising urban grain selling price, which could worsen either food availability or accessibility. Under the constraint of central finance, annual fiscal budget for agriculture directly affected the grain works and food security policies in China. In reality, both grain output and price — the two major components in China's food security — demonstrated cyclical trends.

When we rethink China's evolution of food security policies (discussed in earlier sections), the country has experienced roughly four phases of grain reforms since 1978 (Figure 4). Between 1978 and 2003, the output and price of rice evidently demonstrated a reciprocal cyclical pattern. This indicates that fluctuations in China's food security, as reflected in the output and price, are constrained by an important

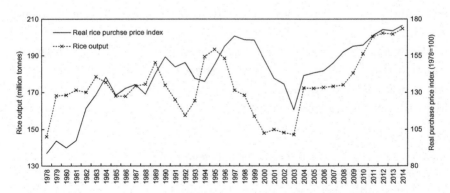

Figure 4: China's Rice Production and Changes in the Real Purchase Price Changes

Source: Du Jun and C. King, "Unravelling China's Food Security Puzzle, 1979–2008", EAI Working Paper no. 167, 2016.

underlying factor, namely the government finance. In other words, output and price changes in grain are restricted by two competing concerns over food security — i.e. fiscal capacity vs. food availability and accessibility.

Between 1978 and 1984, for example, the government's first priority was to maximise grain output in order to enhance food security. However, as the government was then still recovering from the effects of the Cultural Revolution, its fiscal capacity had been seriously constrained. Thus, when China's grain output reached the first post-reform peak in 1983, the central government decided to reduce grain purchase price to balance its finance in what was known as the first significant grain reform — the 1984 grain reform.

From 1984 to 1993, grain prices became the main focus of China's food security policies. On the one hand, the central needed to use grain price to stimulate output to quickly recover from the post-1985 slowdown. On the other hand, the government tried to overcome the difficulties caused by soaring grain prices brought about by high inflation in the late 1980s (Figure 3). Towards the end of the 1980s, the government raised the urban grain subsidies to ensure food accessibility. In 1990, China had the biggest harvest ever in history. Together, the two circumstances placed great fiscal burden on the central government, eventually forcing the government to terminate the urban grain subsidies.

Between 1993 and 2003, China's grain output and grain prices reached the highest levels. The short-lived 1993 marketisation raised grain prices back to the international level.[12] Following high inflation in the early 1990s, the fast-increasing grain selling price forced the central

---

[12] Before 2003, the 1993 reform was the only pilot trial of a complete marketisation in Chinese agriculture. But due to the high inflation at the end of the 1980s and the early 1990s, urban grain started to soar. To stabilise the selling price of urban grain and food accessibility, at the end of 1993, the central government retrieved all grain purchasing and selling rights from the market. The 1993 marketisation was abolished.

to retrieve its grain monopoly rights from the market. Meanwhile, China established its grain reserve for the first time, as a way to recentralise grain monopoly. Concurrently, although the end of the grain coupon system in 1993 had reduced some fiscal burden on the central finance, the administrative cost of grain monopoly began to expand as deepening marketisation in urban China had caused salaries in government-dominated service sectors to increase. With the third output peak in 1994, the costs of grain circulation reached a record high.

Between 1978 and 2003, China implemented three rounds of reforms in grain circulation as the government maintained its monopoly on pricing and circulation. Due to constraints in the government's fiscal capacity, the Chinese government learnt its lessons to oscillate its emphasis between the two objectives — i.e. stimulating production and improving accessibility. In 2003, after several failed pilot experiments, the government eventually abandoned the state monopoly over grain and relegated the issue of food security largely to the market. Simply put, with the removal of the central finance from the system, food availability was determined by production and food accessibility as enhanced by rising household income.

Concluding Remarks

The implementation of a more comprehensive liberalisation and marketisation of the grain sector in the post-2003 had led to several outcomes. First, output recovered rapidly and soon surpassed previous peaks. In the case of rice, output rose by 32.73% between 2003 and 2014, and reached a new historical high in 2014 (Figure 4). Second, prices surged alongside the increase in output. Real grain price reached the fourth peak level in 2012 (Figure 3, Panel *(b)*). The rapidly rising grain prices once again alarmed the central government, whose determination to enhance food security is as steely as in the previous decades. However, by 2012, the government had already abolished most of its monopolistic control over grain production and circulation. Although the central government was no longer constrained as much by its financial conditions, it did not have as many policy instruments to carry out its plans either.

As a result, the government places emphasis on grain reserve, seemingly the only remaining tool. By building up grain reserve, the government believes it can effectively intervene in the market and stabilise grain selling prices. This line of thinking is deemed most appropriate to the current scenario, particularly when the central finance is in good financial health. However, the grain sector, which is largely market-oriented and dependent solely on grain reserve to ensure food security, may face challenges ahead.

First, it is costly to manage a large grain reserve system. Second, a procurement system needs to be put in place in order to build and maintain a certain level of grain reserve. Besides incurring management cost, this system may distort market incentives, leading to higher prices and larger output, which in turn add financial burden to government finance. Third, China's grain sector is becoming increasingly open to the world market. As one of the major buyers on the international market, China's grain purchase may increase international grain prices and weaken food accessibility. Domestic production and prices will also be influenced by changes in the world market. This may, at times, increase market fluctuation and uncertainties, and complicate the management of grain reserve.

Last but not least, improving grain accessibility to poor households is still an issue. Overall, as average household income has risen considerably in the recent decades and expenditure on food only constitutes a small portion of household expenditure, the problem of accessibility is not a serious one. However, the issue remains for families that bear the brunt of rising income inequality. It is therefore imperative that an effective subsistence support system with a comprehensive coverage is put in place.

Chapter 9

The Prospect of China's Renewed State-Owned Enterprise Reforms

Sarah Y TONG*

New Efforts to Reform SOEs Confront Many Challenges

In November 2013, a grand reform blueprint, the "Decision on Major Issues Concerning Comprehensively Deepening Reforms" (hereafter the Decision) was promulgated at the Third Plenary Session of the Communist Party of China's (CPC) 18th Central Committee. Reforming China's state-owned enterprises (SOEs) was featured prominently in the document, stimulating much discussion and excitement among scholars and the general public. Roughly two years later, on 13 September 2015, the "Guideline to Deepen SOE Reforms" (Guideline henceforth) was announced jointly by the Party's Central Committee and the State Council, stirring up a new wave of debate on the prospect of the reforms and the future role of the state sector.

China's SOE reforms started in the late 1970s and have undergone several phases. Most significantly, the reforms in the 1990s produced evident improvement in the state sector by reducing their number and enhancing their business performances. As a group, however, China's

---

*Sarah Y TONG is Senior Research Fellow at the East Asian Institute, National University of Singapore.

SOEs remain poorly governed and seriously inefficient when compared to non-SOEs. State-owned Assets Supervision and Administration Commission (SASAC), the government agency created to oversee the development and reform of SOEs, also failed to either exercise effective supervision or promote much serious reforms. As some SOEs grew larger and made huge profits largely due to their monopolist positions, they have developed into entrenched interest groups with powerful political influence. Corruption becomes rampant, prompting public demands for reinvigorating SOE reforms.

Expectation of further SOE reforms was markedly elevated in late 2013 when the Decision was announced. Regarded as the Party's efforts to reconfigure the relationship between the state and the market, the Decision placed much emphasis on SOE reforms. However, the document generated only limited optimism for a number of reasons. First, it sent conflicting signals on the role of the market and the state: while encouraging the market to play a decisive role in the allocation of resources, it stresses that the state sector would remain the pillar of the economy.

Second, the Decision identified several "new" emphases for SOE reforms, such as the shift from asset management towards capital management and the advancement of mixed ownership, which were not new. The lack of specific measures raised doubt on whether the reforms could overcome difficulties encountered in previous reform efforts. The Guideline further heightened the conceptual contradictions on the direction and principle of China's SOE reforms. It remains unclear whether SOEs are to be purely business entities or they have to also shoulder certain political responsibilities such as exercise administrative control of strategic industries.

Another core concern is with the Party's role in SOEs. Shortly after the announcement of the Guideline in September 2015, CPC Central Committee's General Office publicised the "Opinions on Adhering to the Party's Leadership and Strengthening Party Building in Deepening SOE Reforms". While the Guideline indicates that the authority intends to curb corruption by strengthening the Party's influence and direct participation in SOEs' governance, this seems inconsistent with the overall reform direction, which is to reinforce the market's decisive role and enable the SOEs to be more adaptive, market-oriented, modern and international.

Nevertheless, the Guideline has made some progress in certain areas, including the promotion of rules-based corporate governance to reduce excessive government interference in SOEs' business operations and the introduction of a dual-track system which applies to both the firms and the management teams in SOE governance. The SOEs will be categorised into two groups: commercial ones and those in public services. Commercial SOEs will be further divided into those in competitive sectors and those in various special sectors. Likewise, top managers will also be recruited either from the market or through Party and government recommendations, each with different pay packages and career prospects. There is also indication that the government intends to shift from asset management to capital management by setting up state capital investment companies and state capital management companies. By inserting a layer of investment companies between SOEs and government agencies, such as the SASAC, the reform aims to enhance SOEs' market orientation and reduce bureaucratic meddling.

Great uncertainty remains about the future of China's new round of SOE reforms. Most importantly, the conceptual dilemma regarding the role of the SOEs seems unresolved. As SOE conglomerates become larger and more influential with entrenched interest groups, any serious reform will become operationally difficult and politically risky. Furthermore, since China's SOEs are under the management of many different organs and at different levels of government, reforms can easily be sidetracked by either bureaucratic infighting or indifference.

Previous SOE Reforms and Their Pitfalls

Despite multiple problems, China has made significant advancement in reforming its SOEs since the late 1970s. The government's efforts to transform the state sector had gone through several phases, with different objectives and tactics. During the early years of reforms, the key was to increase managerial autonomy and introduce market incentives to the SOEs. In July 1979, the State Council issued "Provisions Concerning the Expansion of Managerial Autonomy of State-owned (and managed) Enterprises". In April 1983, the government announced "Trial Measures on Shifting Profit Delivery to Tax Submission for State-owned (and managed) Enterprises" where SOEs were required to pay a profit tax of 55% in place of profit delivery. In May 1984, the "Interim Provisions on Further Expanding the Autonomy of State-owned (and managed) Industrial Enterprises" was circulated to further decentralise decision-making.[1]

From the mid-1980s to early 1990s, the key was to introduce a contract system similar to the household responsibility system in rural reforms. In October 1984, the Third Plenum of CPC's 12th Central Committee adopted the "Decision on Economic Reform", which specified SOE reforms as an implementation to separate state ownership from management and to allow SOEs to become autonomous, financially self-reliant legal entities. The experiments of management contract system lasted for a number of years with mixed outcome. A central problem is that while the SOEs were strongly incentivised, effective monitoring was lacking. "Although there is a separation between ownership and managerial autonomy, the absence of the nominal owner means that there is a lack of effective restraint on the managers. In many cases, managerial autonomy was used to pursue personal gain or the interests of small groups of people. Meanwhile, the prevalence of SOEs controlled by insiders leads to a loss of state assets".[2]

A more comprehensive SOE reform plan was promulgated in late 1993 when the "Decision on the Establishment of a Socialist Market Economic System" was approved at the Third Plenum of CPC's 14th Central Committee. It pointed out that the direction of SOE reform was to establish a modern corporate system with "well-defined property

---

[1] See <http://www.people.com.cn/GB/historic/0713/2302.html> (accessed 1 October 2015).

[2] "SOE Reforms: The Path, Core Problems, and The Way Out (Guoqi gaige de lujing, zhengjie he chulu)", 13 May 2014, <http://www.reformdata.org/special/639/> (accessed 29 September 2015).

rights, clear responsibilities, separation of business management from political affairs, and scientific management". Pilot programmes started in 1994 in selected enterprises at both centrally administered and locally administered SOEs. In 1994, the CPC's Fifth Plenum of the 14th Central Committee stipulated that the government would focus on enhancing the state sector by "grasping the large and deregulating the small".

Most significantly, a "Decision of CPC's Central Committee on Major Issues Concerning SOE Reform and Development (the 1999 Decision)" was announced in September 1999 at the Fourth Plenum of CPC's 15th Central Committee. This has been considered the most important and comprehensive document directing China's SOE reforms. It identified two sets of objectives, the short-term and the medium-term ones. The short-term objectives include pulling all loss-making SOEs out of financial difficulties and establishing modern corporate systems in major large and medium-sized SOEs. In the medium term, by 2010, the government aimed "to complete basically the strategic adjustment and restructuring of the SOEs, to establish a relatively perfect modern enterprise system, to improve significantly economic efficiency, to enhance SOEs' technological capability, competitiveness and the ability to withstand market risks, and to enable the state sector to play a leading role in the economy".[3]

The 1999 Decision was also considered the boldest in advocating numerous sweeping changes in SOEs. To "produce high-quality manager", for example, it stresses that "the reform of SOEs' personnel system needs to be deepened" through "combining party recommendation with open market recruitment", and eliminating the equivalent rankings of SOEs and their leaders.

SOE reforms since the late 1990s had produced more pronounced results. While tens of millions of SOE employees were laid off and trillions of non-performing assets removed from the SOEs, the reforms turned around two-thirds of the loss-making SOEs. Large SOEs were consolidated, slashing the number of SOEs and firms with state control

---

[3] See <http://cpc.people.com.cn/GB/64162/71380/71382/71386/4837883.html> (accessed 30 June 2016).

in the industrial sector from 65,000 in 1998 to 27,000 in 2005, or from a share of 39% to 10% during the same period.[4] Meanwhile, the reform agenda was not fully implemented due in part to fierce criticism of certain practices. In particular, some SOE managers obtained state assets through management buy-out (MBO) schemes at very low cost or even for free, raising serious concerns about asset stripping of SOEs. These had led to strong public outcry and hot debates among intellectuals. Consequently, the de facto privatisation of small and medium-sized SOEs through MBO was all but abandoned in 2004 when the government issued stricter rules and regulations.

A New Push to Revive SOE Reforms

Since the early 2000s, little progress had been made in SOE reforms. One development was the establishment of the SASAC[5] in 2003. SASAC was tasked with three responsibilities, as the owner and the regulator of the SOEs, as well as the institution responsible for promoting SOE reforms. While large state-owned industrial conglomerates[6] were placed under the supervision of the SASAC, provincial SASACs were set up to oversee SOEs at different localities.

SASAC has made very limited advancement in fulfilling its responsibilities as the three roles provide conflicting incentives. First, as a representative of state ownership, SASAC has not strongly pushed profitable SOEs to surrender their profits to state treasury, even as many centrally administered SOEs have become hugely profitable. Second, as a regulator, SASAC and its leaders were not given sufficient authority to supervise some powerful SOEs. On the one hand, at vice-ministerial

---

[4] Sarah Y Tong and Huang Yanjie, "China's State-owned Enterprises in the Post-crisis Era: Development and Dilemma", *EAI Background Brief*, no. 694, 3 February 2012.
[5] SOEs in the industry and construction are under the regulation of SASAC, while those in the financial sector are under the supervision of the China Banking Regulatory Commission or China Insurance Regulatory Commission.
[6] Many of these conglomerates were industrial ministry-turned-corporations, which kept their ministerial rankings for the companies and their leaders.

level, SASAC and its leaders were at a lower rank than some ministerial-level SOEs. On the other hand, top executives in some central SOEs were appointed not by SASAC but by the Party's Organisation Department. Third, as the supervisor of the SOEs, SASAC has little incentive to reform the SOEs and to reduce their size and influence. Meanwhile, some SOEs have become hugely profitable, especially the centrally administered ones due in large part to their monopolistic positions and generous government financing. In 2013, SOEs' total profit amounted to RMB2.6 trillion, from less than RMB500 million in 2003. A large majority of SOEs' profits are made by central SOEs, whose share in total rose from 63% in the years 2002 to 2007 to 68% during the 2008–2015 period (Figure 1).

SOEs and state-controlled firms have certainly grown in size. The average number of employees had more than doubled between 1996 and 2014.[7] Total assets per firm surged even more drastically from RMB60

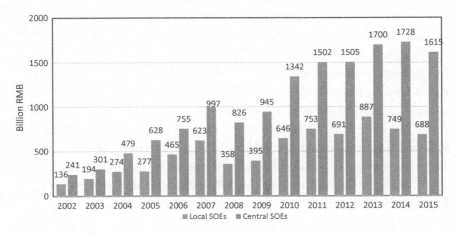

Figure 1:   Profit of Centrally and Locally Managed SOEs

Source: CEIC Data Manager and Sarah Y Tong and Huang Yanjie, "China's State-owned Enterprises in the Post-crisis Era: Development and Dilemma", *EAI Background Brief*, no. 694, 3 February 2012.

---

[7]The numbers cited in this chapter were calculated by the author using data from CEIC Data Manager, unless otherwise specified.

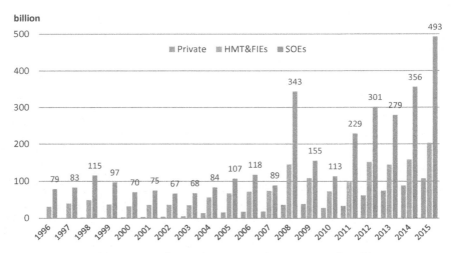

Figure 2: Total Amount of Loss by Loss-making Firms of Different Groups, 1996–2015

Source: CEIC Data Manager.

billion in 1996 to nearly RMB2 trillion in 2014. However, SOEs as a whole remained inefficiently managed, compared to non-SOEs. For example, between 1998 and 2015, the number of industrial enterprises had more than doubled, while the share of loss-making firms more than halved, from 29% to 13%. Among the various groups of firms by ownership types, the state sector fared the worst. In 2015, loss-making firms made up 30% of SOEs, compared unfavourably to 10% for private firms and 22% for firms with non-mainland investment. Total losses by loss-making SOEs surged to RMB343 billion during the 2008 global economic crisis. In 2015, it amounted to RMB493 billion, 1.6 times the combined amount of private firms (RMB107 billion) and firms with non-mainland investment (RMB203 billion) (Figure 2).

Investment in the state sector has thus generated the least amount of profit, compared to that of other firms. Figure 3 shows that SOEs' performance had deteriorated in recent years, albeit better than in the 1990s. They are significantly less capable than private and foreign-invested firms in generating profit from their investment and the gap

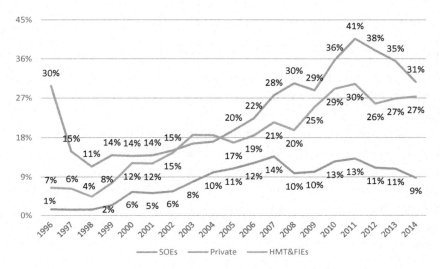

Figure 3:   Profit to Fixed Ratio, 1996–2014

Note: HMT denotes Hong Kong-Macao-Taiwan.
Source: CEIC Data Manager.

between them is widening.[8] Meanwhile, there has been little progress in SOE reforms identified in the 1999 Decision, such as further "separation of enterprises from government". Likewise, the administrative ranking of top SOE executives remains.

SOEs have been criticised in many areas. Many believe that China's SOEs are badly run due to poor corporate governance and market monopoly; they are less efficient than non-SOEs, resulting in overall lower economic performance. With their privileged positions, SOEs also crowded out non-state firms in financing and posed unfair competition in the market. As some monopolistic SOEs become larger and enjoy more profit, the prevalence of vested interests arouse resentment from not only the public but also within the government. For example, some highly profitable SOEs had resisted proposals to

---

[8] According to a study by the UniRule Institute of Economics, "The Nature, Performance and Reform of the State-owned Enterprises" (2011), the real rate of return to capital for China's SOEs was not only low but sometimes negative, if the full scale of subsidies including subsidised capital, land and energy were taken into account.

increase the contribution rate of SOE profit to the Ministry of Finance. In 2010, SASAC issued an order requiring central SOEs to withdraw from the real estate sector, but the order was largely ignored. What further puts the state sector in a bad light is its high incidence of corruption. High-profile corruption cases are rampant in the top management of large SOEs.

China's SOEs evidently require deeper reforms, which had been highlighted repeatedly in the much lauded 2013 Decision. Despite much comprehensive coverage and eloquent deliberation, the Decision remains largely a conceptual design tainted with ambiguities and contradictions in need of further details. As SOE reforms are complex and affect the interests of powerful groups, a clearly stated plan with the top leader's resolve will be essential.

The New Blueprint and its Contradictions

As a medium-term reform blueprint, the essence of the 2013 Decision, many believe, is the Party's efforts to reconfigure the relations between the state and the market. While it has reignited hopes of advancing SOE reforms, many remain doubtful, for mainly two reasons. First, the Decision included conflicting signals regarding the role of the market and the state. It proclaimed for the first time that the market would play a "decisive role" in the allocation of resources and the state would refrain from excessive intervention in the economy. However, the Decision also stressed that the state sector would remain the pillar of the economy and that it would "continually strengthen the vitality, control and influence of the public sector". It further stated that "China's basic economic system is one with public ownership as its main body but allowing for the development of all types of ownership". Such ambiguity causes confusion and serious doubt.

Second, the Decision indicated new directions of SOE reforms but left out the much-needed details. For example, the Decision highlighted that it would shift its emphasis from asset management to capital management in state assets supervision. While it has indicated its preference for Singapore's Temasek-styled model, it is unclear how this is to be executed at the operational level.

In September 2015, after several rounds of revision and much public anticipation, the government finally issued the Guideline on Deepening SOE Reforms. Despite the broad coverage and comprehensive discussion, the Guideline only further heightened the conceptual contradictions of the direction and principle of China's SOE reforms. At the same time, a clear definition of China's SOEs is lacking, especially whether they are business entities or whether and to what extent they also have political responsibilities for the Party. If SOEs are considered special entities, it would be difficult to sustain a level playing field for firms to compete fairly and openly in the marketplace. To some, "the objectives of China's SOEs are not only profit maximization, other political goals such as control of core strategic industries, price control, employment generation, and social responsibility are also important".[9]

The role of the Party is another central concern. The Guideline indicates that the government intends to curb corruption by strengthening the Party's influence in the SOEs. It calls for "the full play of Party organization's political central role in the SOEs and a clear designation of Party organization's legal status in SOEs' corporate governance structure". More specifically, it proposes the principle of "four simultaneous and two cross-overs". The four "simultaneous" literally means that "the SOE reforms will be promoted while insisting on simultaneous planning of Party building, on simultaneous establishment of Party organization and working bodies, on simultaneous assignment of party branch leaders and staff, and on simultaneous launching of Party work".

Moreover, the government aims to "uphold and improve the two-way access and the cross-representation system for SOEs leadership". The Guideline states that "eligible members of the Party leadership can be members of SOEs' board of directors, board of supervisors, or

---

[9] See <http://m.21jingji.com/article/20150916/1154ef09b8059813a503fee07c26
20a2.html> (accessed 17 September 2015).

managers, through legal procedures". Conversely, "members of the board of directors, board of supervisors, and top executives can have an appropriate degree of cross-representation with members of SOEs' Party leadership…Generally, SOEs' Party secretary general and the chairman of the board are to be held by the same person".

Most recently, an article authored by the Party Committee of China's SASAC of the State Council on "Strengthening Party Building in the Comprehensive Deepening of SOE Reforms"[10] in the 求是 (*Qiu Shi*) journal caused serious concerns on the direction of China's SOE reforms. Most conspicuous of the writing is the assertion that "major decisions (of the SOEs) must first be examined by the Party committees (or leading Party group) of the enterprises, which then propose their opinions and suggestions. SOEs' major operational and managerial matters involving regulations of national macroeconomy, national strategies, national security and so on must first be discussed and approved by their Party committees (or leading party groups) before a decision is made by the board of directors and the executive team".

Such consolidation of the Party's direct participation in SOEs' governance seems inconsistent with the overall reform direction, which aims to strengthen the market's decisive role and to enable the SOEs to be more adaptive, market-oriented, modern and international. It is also unclear how widely applicable these principles will be as the government also promotes mixed ownership reforms for SOEs. In fact, the Guideline stipulates that "the establishment of Party organizations and the carrying out of Party work is the prerequisite for SOEs' mixed-ownership reforms".

Meanwhile, "the type of establishment, the allocation of responsibilities, and the mode of management for these Party organization will be determined scientifically according to the characteristics of the mixed-ownership SOEs". Such rules will undoubtedly increase anxieties of private entrepreneurs on whether these SOEs with mixed ownership can avoid the Party's administrative interference.

---

[10] See <http://www.qstheory.cn/dukan/qs/2016-05/31/c_1118938354.htm> (accessed 26 June 2016).

Moreover, without transparency, it remains uncertain how these rules could help curb corruption in the SOEs.

Breakthroughs and Compromises

Compared to the Decision, the Guideline has made some degrees of advancement and breakthroughs in selected areas. However, these advancements are often enfeebled by evident compromises. First, the Guideline stresses the promotion of rules-based corporate governance which is important for "mixed ownership" reforms. The key however is in its execution. An obvious test of this principle is how SOEs' top executives will be appointed. In the past, for example, leaders of the SOEs were often decided by CPC's Organisation Department, leaving the board of directors as a dummy in the process. Whether such practices will be stopped based on the new Guideline is still unknown.

Second, following the principles highlighted in the Decision, the Guideline further clarifies that SOEs are to be classified into broadly two categories, commercial and public service, and managed differently. Commercial SOEs will be further grouped into those in fully competitive sectors and those in various special areas, such as national security and national economic lifeline, and those delegated with major government projects. For SOEs in fully competitive sectors, the government allows a more flexible ownership participation where "the state may have either absolute or relative control, or as a minority shareholder". For SOEs in special areas, the government pledges to "maintain state capital's control". Consequently, the extent of SOE reform will depend largely on how broad these special areas are defined. The wider the special areas, less reforms may be expected. Another key question is how and by whom these categorisations of SOEs are determined.

Third, on personnel management of SOEs' top executives, the Guideline introduced a dual-track system, one for Party cadres and the other for professional managers. Those under the system of Party cadres will keep their administrative rank level at lower salary than professional managers, but continue to receive benefit equivalent to those in the government bureaucracy while retaining their path back to the government and Party organs. In particular, the Guideline specifies that the government will "make clear the channel for existing management to switch toward professional managers", indicating that SOE executives can choose between the two. This seems a clear compromise and a step back from the 1999 reform agenda, which stated that administrative ranks were to be abandoned for SOEs and their top executives. The dual-track system may also prove to be difficult in practice.

Fourth, the Guideline includes lengthy discussion on the shift in SOE management approach from asset management to capital management. The government aims to "scientifically define the boundaries of government supervision as investor of the asset, to delegate controls that are beyond its designated rights according to the law, and never to over-step". More specifically, to distant SOEs from SASAC, the Guideline proposes the establishment of state capital investment companies and state capital management companies (the Temasek model). As these investment and management companies are considered more market-oriented and entrepreneurial, the proposed arrangement is intended to better evade the government's interventionist tendencies towards SOEs. In practice, this means adding a new layer between SASAC and the SOEs. It is unclear whether this will indeed reduce bureaucratic interference or conversely increase administrative burden and create new complexities.

The shift from asset management to capital management also aims "to dispose state asset with fair market-valuation, to change the form of the state asset, and to reallocate the cashed out asset toward more desirable sectors and industries". This indicates that, in the future, more state-owned assets may be transferred or sold to pay debt or fill the shortfalls in the government's social security system.

The Guideline also promotes more flexibility in SOE's ownership structure and identifies several new forms of ownership reforms. It states that "for enterprises that require 100% state ownership, other state capital should be actively encouraged to participate so as to diversify stock holdings". Moreover, the Guideline supports ownership structure reforms at the level of the industrial conglomerates, "creating conditions to achieve the stock listing for the overall groups".

The government will "allow some state capital to be converted to preferred shares and explore a management system for such special shares in certain specific sectors".

These proposals to diversify SOEs ownership structure aim to strengthen governance and improve efficiency through the introduction of more and varied investors. It may also help protect the SOEs from excessive interference from the government. Meanwhile, the adoption of preferred shares can be an effective tool to safeguard key national interest. However, as detailed rules have not been announced, much remain unclear. For example, the possible cross-ownership of SOEs may lead to more, rather than less, government interference.

The Guideline also places emphasis on the strategic reorganisation of the SOEs. The reforms of the late 1990s, especially the "grasp the large and let go of the small" approach, have greatly reduced the number of SOEs. Since the establishment of the SASAC in 2003, the centrally administered SOEs have been reduced further to 112.

The Guideline suggests that the government will "promote the concentration of state capital toward important sectors and key areas concerning national security, national economic lifeline, and people's livelihood, as well as key infrastructure projects; toward forward-looking and strategic industries; and toward SOEs with core competitiveness". More mergers of centrally administered SOEs, leading to further reduction in their numbers could be expected.

Future SOE Reforms Remain Uncertain

Great uncertainty for future SOE reforms remains for a number of reasons. The general direction is unclear and inconsistent. With SOE conglomerates becoming increasingly larger in size and more influential with entrenched interest groups, drastic reforms would be very difficult at the operational level and politically risky. This is especially true when economic oligarchs are associated with political factions.

Furthermore, as China's SOEs are under the management of many different government jurisdictions and at different levels of governments, reforms can easily be sidetracked by bureaucratic infighting. The current leadership also faces a more general problem of bureaucratic inaction due partly to the ongoing anti-corruption campaign. As such, China's SOE reforms will likely be a slow process, with trials and errors along the way.

There has been little progress with respect to SOE reforms since November 2013 when the Decision was announced. Although there were changes concerning SOE governance, they were generally of piecemeal measures rather than serious reforms. For example, when the high executive pay of SOE managers was widely criticised, the government issued new rules to cut executives' pay in certain large SOEs. Such administrative measures are no solution to SOE's incentive and governance problem.

On mixed ownership reform for SOEs, the approach taken was cautious although it was highlighted in the Decision as a key measure of SOE reforms. It states that for SOEs' mixed ownership reforms, "(the government) will not engage in arbitrary matchmaking, (the reform) will not be extended to all SOEs, there is no timetable, and (the reform of each SOE) will only proceed when the condition is ripe". The government also pledged that "in order to prevent the loss of state assets, the reform will strictly follow the procedures and adhere to (the principle of) openness and fairness". These general principles have not been substantiated as no details were given as to what constitute the loss of state assets and how such losses can be avoided.

The biggest issue is probably that of the contradiction between monopoly and fair competition. The Decision included an exceptionally strong statement: "the state shall protect the property rights and legal interest of economic entities with various ownership forms; ensure that they enjoy equal rights under the law in the use of production factors, that they participate in open, fair, and equitable market competition, and that they enjoy the same legal protection". The details were again lacking. The Guideline further stressed that SOE reforms shall "make the SOEs stronger, better, and bigger so as to enhance the state sector's vitality, dominance, and influence". This suggests that the government does not intend to seriously weaken SOEs' monopoly.

Chapter 10

Made in China 2025: A Grand Strategy for Industrial Upgrading

Sarah Y TONG and KONG Tuan Yuen*

From Strategic Emerging Industries to Made in China 2025

As China's economy enters the state of "new normal" characterised by a slowdown, the government is eager to facilitate industrial restructuring and committed to explore new growth engines. Indeed, industrial upgrading is featured heavily in the Proposal for 13th Five-Year Programme (2015–2020) that will lead China to achieve its goal of attaining the status of a moderately prosperous society by 2020.

China's industrial policies form an important part of the government's overall development strategies and have evolved considerably over the past decades. From the late 1970s to the 2000s, the emphasis shifted from labour-intensive sectors to the technology-intensive sectors in promoting key strategic industries, such as eco-friendly and energy-saving industries. The strategic emerging industries were first proposed by the Hu Jintao–Wen Jiabao administration and later

* Sarah Y TONG is Senior Research Fellow at the East Asian Institute, National University of Singapore; and KONG Tuan Yuen is Visiting Research Fellow at the same institute.

incorporated into the 12th Five-Year Plan in 2011, which identified seven industries to spur industrial restructuring, facilitate economic transformation and enhance global competitiveness. The seven strategic emerging industries included energy-efficient and environmental technologies, new-generation information technology, biotechnology, high-end equipment manufacturing, new energy, new materials and new-energy vehicles.

In line with the global economic restructuring and environmental constraints that have hindered domestic industrialisation, the Chinese government initiated the Made in China 2025 plan at the 2015 *lianghui* (the two meetings of the National People's Congress and the Chinese People's Political Consultative Conference) in early March and promulgated by Premier Li Keqiang subsequently on 19 May 2015. The preparation of the ambitious plan was led by the Ministry of Industry and Information Technology (MIIT) and took over two years. More than 20 government ministries and departments took part, including the National Development and Reform Commission, Ministry of Science and Technology, Ministry of Finance, and General Administration of Quality Supervision and Inspection, with input from over 150 experts from China Academy of Engineering.[1]

The seven strategic emerging industries highlighted in 2011 were expanded to 10 key sectors in the Made in China 2025 plan (Table 1). The automated machine tools and robotics industry was included for the first time to promote automation and intelligent factories. More importantly, the innovation-driven strategy has an important role in the 13th Five-Year Plan in propping up the development of key sectors. Of noteworthy is the emphasis of the service role in manufacturing, such as service-embedded manufacturing and producer services, in the Made in China 2025 plan.

The Made in China 2025 plan is different from the previous industrial policies in several aspects. It is a long-term, high-level and grand

---

[1] "Press Conference by Su Bo on 'Made in China 2015'", 30 March 2015, at <http://news.xinhuanet.com/info/2015-03/30/c_134108773.htm> (accessed 26 June 2016).

Table 1:   The 10 Key Sectors in the Made in China 2025 Plan

1. The next-generation new information technology;

2. Automated machine tools and robotics;

3. Aerospace and aeronautical equipment;

4. Maritime equipment and high-tech shipping;

5. Advanced rail transport equipment;

6. New-energy vehicles and equipment;

7. Power equipment;

8. Agricultural machinery;

9. New materials; and

10. Biomedical and advanced medical devices

Source: The State Council of The People's Republic of China, "Made in China 2025", 19 May 2015, at <http://www.gov.cn/zhengce/content/2015-05/19/content_9784.htm> (accessed 30 June 2016).

industrial strategy that highlights not only the traditional industries but also the development of advanced industries and modern services. With this initiative, the Chinese government hopes to transform China from a world manufacturer to a world manufacturing superpower by combining government fund and market-driven technology revolution and innovation. According to the government, the Made in China 2025 plan is the first 10-year action plan designed to transform China from a manufacturing giant into a world manufacturing power. It will be followed by two other plans in order to achieve the eventual goal of making China the world's leading manufacturing power by 2049, which will also be the 100th anniversary of the founding of the People's Republic of China.[2]

The Made in China 2025 plan, which aims to restructure China's manufacturing sector, constitutes an essential part of China's overall economic transformation from an investment-driven and export-oriented growth to one that is innovation-driven and consumption-oriented. Enhancing the overall competitiveness of the manufacturing sector is also

---

[2]"Made in China 2025", 19 May 2015, at <http://www.gov.cn/zhengce/content/2015-05/19/content_9784.htm> (accessed 26 June 2016).

the plan's primary objective. In addition, the plan is the first of a three-step grand strategy that serves to bridge the immense gap between China and the world's leading countries in technology development. China foresees that the world is undergoing a new round of industrial revolution and aspires to join the top league in the coming decades.

Certainly, the Made in China 2025 initiative will face many challenges. First, the direction and progress of technological advancement and innovation would be debatable due to the controversial industry policy. Second, lack of effective coordination among government institutions and various policy implementations, and excessive state intervention may hinder the success of a comprehensive and long-term initiative. Third, the plan, being an overriding guideline, lacks the specifics — there is heavy focus on the objectives and principles but ambiguity on how it is to be implemented.

The Rationale behind and Objectives of Made in China 2025 Plan

The rapid expansion of the manufacturing industry has significantly helped sustain China's growth over the last decades and remains essential to China future growth. As the manufacturing sector is considered the pillar of the national economy, its continued development and improvement are therefore vital. These are the fundamentals that underlie the Made in China 2025 strategic plan.

The rationale behind the plan is explained as follows. First, China's economy has entered the so-called "new normal" phase, as evident from a growth deceleration. As the Chinese government fine-tunes the fiscal and monetary policies to ensure macroeconomic stability, initiating strategies in search of new sources of growth is imperative. Hence, the Made in China 2025 plan — aimed at upgrading the overall manufacturing industry towards the technological frontier — presents the prospect of leading China onto a technology-driven development trajectory.

Second, in the face of increasing competition from both emerging and advanced economies, it is imperative that China strengthens the overall competitiveness of the manufacturing sector. As factor prices rise, China is losing its competitive edge to some emerging economies, such as Vietnam, Cambodia and Bangladesh. Meanwhile, competition from other advanced economies has also intensified in recent years as they stepped up efforts to reindustrialise. China is under pressure to propel its industrial restructuring and move its manufacturing up the global value chain. It needs to upgrade the industrial structure by developing competitive high-end industries such as high-value equipment manufacturing.

Third, to become one of the world's top manufacturing powers, China needs to narrow the technological gap with developed countries. Despite being a manufacturing giant, China still lags behind leading advanced countries in technology and innovation. The Made in China 2025 plan is deemed an important enabler of China's aspiration to achieve industrialisation and modernisation equivalent to those of Germany and Japan to rank among world's advanced manufacturing powers.[3] Indeed, China as a manufacturer is still weak in terms of core technology and innovation. The Made in China 2025 plan aims to transform China from the world's largest manufacturer to the world's strongest manufacturer. As the world undergoes a new round of global technological and industrial revolution, this offers China an opportunity to step into high-end manufacturing by producing and exporting high-quality heavy-duty equipment.

The Made in China 2025 plan, issued on 19 May 2015 by the State Council, can be viewed as a comprehensive initiative that covers a wide range of manufacturing sectors. The goal is to systematically upgrade and transform Chinese industry into a leading manufacturing superpower, with higher efficiency and productivity, and repute in innovation and brand recognition.

China proposes a "three-step" strategy to achieve its grand objectives, setting specific goals to be materialised within 10 years for each and every step. Step one, by 2025, China aims to join the league of major manufacturing powers; step two, by 2035, China aims to attain comparative ranking among the major manufacturing powers; step

---

[3] "Core of Made in China 2025 Strategy: Innovation", *CCTV.com*, 13 May 2015, at <http://english.cntv.cn/2015/05/13/ARTI1431503542623865.shtml> (accessed 3 October 2016).

three, by the 100th anniversary of the founding of the People's Republic of China in 2049, China aims to emerge as a leading manufacturing superpower. The specific targets set for all three steps include criteria, such as innovation capability, quality and efficiency, digitalisation of industries and green development (Table 2).[4]

The plan also highlights four main principles in the future development of China's manufacturing sector. First, adopt a market-oriented approach under government guidance; second, take a long-term perspective in development, capitalising on the present as a starting point; third, advance manufacturing as a whole with major breakthroughs made in key areas; and fourth, promote both indigenous development and win-win cooperation.[5]

In addition, the government outlines five guidelines to promote innovative development of the manufacturing industry — innovation-driven, quality as top priority, green development, structure optimisation and talent development. The government initiates five tasks in line with the five guidelines: setting up a national innovation centre for manufacturing; promoting intelligent manufacturing; strengthening the industrial base; promoting green manufacturing; and innovating in high-end equipment manufacturing.

To achieve the objectives, the five guidelines are further itemised into nine priority tasks: (i) improve the innovative capacity in manufacturing sector; (ii) deepen the integration between information technology and industry; (iii) strengthen the basic industrial capability; (iv) build and foster Chinese brands; (v) enforce green manufacturing; (vi) promote breakthroughs in 10 key sectors; (vii) advance the restructure of manufacturing sector; (viii) promote service-oriented manufacturing and manufacturing-related services; and (ix) internationalise manufacturing.

---

[4] "'Made in China 2025' to Concentrate on 10 Key Sectors", 22 May 2015, at <http://chineseportal.net/news/article/made-in-china-2025-to-concentrate-on-ten-key-sectors> (accessed 29 June 2016).

[5] "Made in China 2025", 19 May 2015, at <http://www.gov.cn/zhengce/content/2015-05/19/content_9784.htm> (accessed 1 July 2016).

Table 2: Main Manufacturing Indices, 2020 and 2025

Categories	Indices	2013	2015	2020	2025
Innovation Capability	R&D/Sales ratio	0.88	0.95	1.26	1.68
	Number of invention patents per 100 million yuan sales revenue	0.36	0.44	0.70	1.10
Quality and Efficiency	Quality competitiveness index[a]	83.1	83.5	84.5	85.5
	Rate increase of manufacturing value-add	—	—	2% higher than in 2015	4% higher than in 2015
	Labour Productivity Growth	—	—	± 7.5 (Average Growth Rate of 13th Five- Year Plan)	± 6.5 (Average Growth Rate of 14th Five- Year Plan)
Digitalisation of Industry	High-speed internet access (%)[b]	37	50	70	82
	Digital research and development, and design tool penetration rate (%)	52	58	72	84
	Digitisation of key manufacturing process (%)[c]	27	33	50	64
Green Development	Reduction in energy consumption	—	—	18% lower than in 2015	34% lower than in 2015
	Reduction of CO_2 emission	—	—	22% lower than in 2015	40% lower than in 2015
	Reduction in water consumption	—	—	23% lower than in 2015	41% lower than in 2015
	Comprehensive utilisation of industrial solid waste	62	65	73	79

Note: [a]Quality competitiveness index refers to the overall quality of China's manufacturing industry in terms of technical and economic comprehensive index calculated based on 12 indicators.

[b]High-speed internet access refers to household fixed broadband penetration rate.

[c]Average percentage of digitisation in key manufacturing process of all industrial enterprises.

Source: "Made in China 2025", 19 May 2015, at <http://www.gov.cn/zhengce/content/2015-05/19/content_9784.htm> (accessed 1 July 2016).

Furthermore, the Made in China 2025 plan proposes to support the creation of national manufacturing innovation centres by utilising financial and fiscal tools. The government aims to establish 15 such centres by 2020 and 40 by 2025. The plan also calls for relying on market institutions, strengthening intellectual property rights (IPR) protection for small- and medium-sized enterprises (SMEs), and the effective use of IPR in business strategy.[6] This allows firms to self-declare their own technology and better participate in international technology standards-setting.

The government recognises the problems faced by China's manufacturing sector. These is still a lack of understanding of the importance of innovation in driving development. Moreover, Chinese products are not known for good quality. With such huge number of firms and just a few that possess genuine international competitiveness, the structure of the manufacturing sector is far from ideal. Likewise, China has a large talent pool, but few are capable of leading large multinational firms. Resource and environmental constraints are tightening. China is also in need of new demographic dividends to support development.[7]

Nevertheless, the government believes that China still enjoys four major advantages, including a sizeable domestic market, a large number of enterprises full of vigour and vitality, a long-term development strategy and adequate human resources, with steady supply of qualified personnel and college graduates joining the manufacturing industry.

A Comparative Analysis of the Made in China 2025 Plan

The Made in China 2025 plan may be viewed as a continuation of the numerous industrial policies the government formulated in the past.

---

[6] "Made in China 2025", Center for Strategic and International Studies, 1 June 2015, at <http://csis.org/publication/made-china-2025> (accessed 1 July 2016).

[7] "'Made in China 2025' Announced: The Three Step Strategy to Make Breakthroughs in 10 Key Areas", 19 May 2015, at <http://news.ifeng.com/a/20150519/43789100_0.shtml?f=hao123> (accessed 1 July 2016).

Industrial policies in China have evolved considerably over the decades, due to the Chinese government's incessant effort in restructuring, upgrading and reforming its industry. Different priorities and emphases were introduced at different periods to stimulate the industrial sector.

From the late 1970s to 2000s, there was a shift in emphasis from labour-intensive sectors to technology-intensive sectors in order to promote key strategic industries, such as eco-friendly and energy-saving industries. Between the late 1970s and mid-1980s, the government focused on developing labour-intensive industries. In the 1990s, the push for further industrialisation in tandem with other government objectives, such as reforming the inefficient state sector, encouraged the development of non-state industries and promoted exports.[8] Since the early 2000s, reform has gradually geared towards industrial consolidation and upgrading. While sustaining industrial growth has remained central to China's economy, tackling overcapacity in several industries has become a key objective of China's industrial restructuring.

Under the 12th Five-Year Programme issued in 2012, the government aimed to upgrade traditional industries and laid out seven strategic emerging industries to ensure the sustainability and global competitiveness of Chinese manufacturing industries. The seven strategic emerging industries include new-energy automobile, energy-saving and environmental protection, new-generation information technology, biotechnology, high-end equipment manufacturing, new energy and new material. Interestingly, some of the strategic emerging industries overlap with the 10 key sectors in the Made in China 2025 plan.

However, the unveiling of the Made in China 2025 plan reveals major differences between the current leadership and the previous Hu–Wen administration in their approach to restructuring, innovation and technology upgrading. First, the plan is the first step of a

---

[8] Zheng Yongnian and Sarah Y. Tong, *China's Evolving Industrial Policies and Economic Restructuring*, London and New York, Routledge, 2014.

long-term, strategic and high-level plan that focuses solely on manufacturing and adapting the industry to both international trends and tendencies in domestic economic and social development.[9] The plan not only promotes the transformation and upgrading of China's traditional manufacturing sector, but also responds to the development of new technology revolution in order to realise high-end transformation in modern industries and services. Thus, the Made in China 2025 plan should not be regarded as a conventional industrial planning like the 13th or 14th Five Year Programme.

Second, technology revolution and innovation form the core of the Made in China 2025 plan, which stipulates the guiding principles, general objectives and the development of key areas. The fundamental premise of this plan is to embrace new technology innovations in order to keep pace with the developed world. For instance, there are clear and specific measures for innovation, quality, intelligent manufacturing and green production, with benchmarks identified for 2013 and 2015 and goals set for 2020 and 2025.

Third, market mechanisms are highlighted and identified as the crucial drivers of the plan although there is acknowledgement of state involvement in the plan. For example, there is a shift in focus towards greater effective use of the intellectual property (IP) system to encourage firms to self-declare the technology standards they wish to adopt and participate in the international standards system, instead of following a top-down approach that demands development of unique domestic technical standards in industrial sectors.

Although the Made in China 2025 plan draws direct inspiration from Germany's "Industry 4.0" plan, it differs significantly from its German counterpart. The essence of Industry 4.0 is intelligent manufacturing, i.e. applying the tools of information technology to production. Germany's Industry 4.0 utilises sophisticated technologies to develop a smart, efficient and fully networked manufacturing

---

[9] "Interview with Su Bo, the drafter of <Made in China 2025>", *iNewsweek*, 21 August 2015, at <http://people.inewsweek.cn/detail-2117.html> (accessed 3 October 2016).

process that integrates production, suppliers, business partners and customers.[10]

As the German industry has a strong and advanced technological and industrial base, the application of Industry 4.0 is more straightforward. This primarily involves the use of the internet of things to more efficiently connect SMEs in global production and innovation networks, facilitating mass production and product customisation.

China's industrial development, on the other hand, is highly uneven. The Made in China 2025 plan aims to simultaneously promote industries that are at different levels (i.e. 2.0, 3.0 and 4.0) of development, implying that if high-end industries' transformation and upgrading progress by leaps and bounds, traditional industries must also attain the same to be on a par with the high-end industries. The task is therefore more complex and difficult.

The Challenges Faced in Implementing the Ambitious Plan

The Made in China 2025 plan is ambitious, grand and goal-oriented, typical of any China's plan which faces numerous challenges in implementation and in achieving results. First, it is difficult to gauge and evaluate the direction and progress of technological advancement and innovation. Second, doubt abounds about the effectiveness of government planning and state intervention. Third, the uncertainties surrounding the government's effort probably stem from the lack of implementation details and measures in the plan, such as policy evaluation, financing allocation and human resource management, despite the grand objectives and goals.

The plan stresses the importance of a market-driven innovation with government guidance and a business environment conducive to

---

[10] "Made in China 2025: How Beijing is Revamping Its Manufacturing Sector", 9 June 2015, at <http://www.scmp.com/tech/innovation/article/1818381/made-china-2025-how-beijing-revamping-its-manufacturing-sector> (accessed 2 July 2016).

innovation. Yet, it is unclear how government policy support can serve to enhance innovative activities. For example, most of China's current innovation still focuses on basic research instead of commercialisation and industrialisation. The Chinese State Intellectual Property Office reported that about 95% of the patents filed by colleges and universities are idle and never make it to the marketplace. This is mainly attributed to the fact that the number of patents filed — but not the patent transformation rate — is taken as one of the evaluation criteria of college performance. The Chinese government has therefore injected large amount of research and development (R&D) funding and held many patents over the last decade, but the core technology of new-energy vehicles, i.e. the battery technology, is still mostly imported from foreign countries.

Implementing such an ambitious and comprehensive plan is challenging as coordination among different government agencies is difficult and state intervention yields doubtful result. The plan therefore calls for relying on market institutions, strengthening the IPR protection for SMEs and incorporating IPR in business strategy. However, no concrete measures are put in place to facilitate the necessary institutional changes. Furthermore, some researchers are pessimistic about the plan, believing that the government only gives consideration to "innovation and research as those beneficial to the government".[11] That there is an unfair bias towards funding innovations that are favoured by the government instead of funding those driven by the market, therefore, possibly exists. Likewise, privately owned and foreign-invested firms are probably in a disadvantageous position in applying for funding. Furthermore, in providing funding for innovations, the plan tends to select industries based on predictions of trend and this approach often leads to inefficient or misuse of funding. Indeed, the plan designates 10 priority industries for provision of financial support. Concrete

---

[11] "'Made in China 2025': A New Era for Chinese Manufacturing", 2 September 2015, at <http://knowledge.ckgsb. edu.cn/2015/09/02/technology/made-in-china-2025-a-new-era-for-chinese-manufacturing/> (accessed 2 July 2016).

steps and approaches will, however, only be defined and determined later when new policies formulated to advance the plan are rolled out in the coming years.[12]

The Chinese government had set up a venture capital fund of 40 billion yuan in August 2015 to guide social institutions and companies to invest over 180 billion yuan in key sectors. Most Chinese SMEs and new ventures are in need of funds to improve product quality and operational process or embark on innovation efforts, e.g. use of automation and technology. However, the reality is that they possess few fixed assets to take out mortgage loans from financial institutions. The financial support is eventually channelled to and concentrated in those few larger companies, instead of being evenly distributed across various sectors and enterprises, which consider the funding an incentive for them to explore innovation possibilities.

In June 2015, the State Council established a National Leading Group on the Building of a Manufacturing Power. The sheer number of institutions that this leading group has to engage with attests to the complexity of tasks involved as well as the difficulties in coordinating various relevant policies.

The Chinese government has set up five key projects to promote the development of 10 key sectors and establish targets to be achieved by 2020 and 2025. However, not all of the key sectors are provided with details of the implementation and specific initiatives, thereby making periodic evaluation of performance difficult. Besides, in a fast-changing world, it is meaningless to evaluate a plan five or 10 years after its implementation. To track the progress of key sectors, the Chinese government should attempt to adopt the private sector's practice of evaluation using key performance indicators. On the other hand, according to a survey conducted in China by ManpowerGroup, technical staff, technicians, R&D staff, IT staff and engineers are in high

---

[12] "China's Master Plan to Become a World Manufacturing Power", *The Diplomat*, 20 May 2015, at <http://thediplomat.com/2015/05/chinas-master-plan-to-become-a-world-manufacturing-power/> (accessed 2 July 2016).

demand by strategic emerging industries, but these positions are also among the top 10 most difficult to fill in 2015. Apparently, the Chinese labour market is unable to fulfil the demands of industrial development due to skill shortages. The education system, particularly the advanced vocational education system, is expected to make adjustments rapidly to train and provide sufficient skilled manpower.

Chapter 11

Regional Development in China under Xi Jinping

YU Hong*

Regional Economic Development in China: An Overview

China's regional policies were biased towards the coastal eastern region from the early reform era to the late 1990s. The state policy outlined by the late leader Deng Xiaoping focused on "coastal development strategy" to attract foreign investment in export-oriented manufacturing and boost foreign trade. Unbalanced regional development and widening regional disparity among the eastern, central and western regions are hence serious consequences of the state's distorted regional policy and the geographical factors. China's regional development policies that favour the "coastal development strategy" had resulted in increasing regional economic disparity in terms of gross domestic product (GDP) from the early 1980s to 2002 (Figure 1). The coefficient of variation, as a measurement of spatial inequality, rose to 0.684 in 2002 from 0.470 in 1982 (Figure 2).

China's phenomenal economic growth has largely been concentrated in the coastal eastern area. The three mega global city-clusters — the

---

*YU Hong is Senior Research Fellow at the East Asian Institute, National University of Singapore.

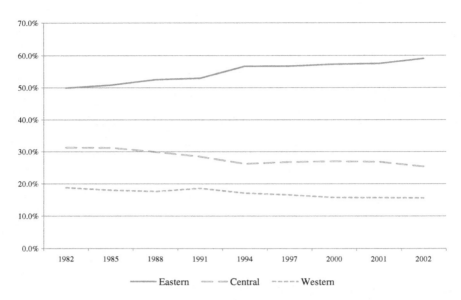

Figure 1: Shares of Eastern, Central and Western Regions in China's Gross Domestic Product (GDP), 1982–2002

Source: Compiled by the author based on National Bureau of Statistics, *China Statistical Yearbook*, China Statistics Press, various years.

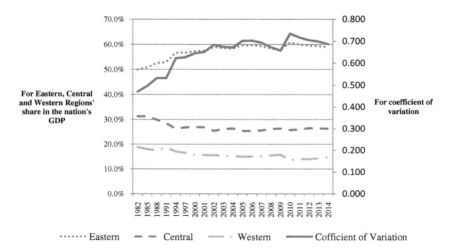

Figure 2: Measurement of Regional Economic Disparity in China, 1982–2014

Source: Compiled by the author based on National Bureau of Statistics, *China Statistical Yearbook*, China Statistics Press, various years.

Pearl River Delta, Yangtze River Delta and the Beijing–Tianjin–Hebei region — are located within the coastal eastern region, and have been transformed into prosperous economic powerhouses based on regional and global competitiveness. The city-clusters have unparalleled advantages of coastal geography, agglomeration of manufacturing industries, abundant resources of human and physical capital, technology and innovation capability over any other regions in China.

Despite China's current status as the world's second-largest economy and the world's largest exporting nation after nearly four decades of reform and opening up, it is burdened with many domestic problems and challenges — imbalanced regional development being one of the most serious. China's conventional development model based on state investment and trade has become increasingly unsustainable. Against this backdrop, regional development disparity becomes an increasingly prominent and worrying issue. China has arrived at a crossroads in determining the direction of future reform, and its Chinese leaders are also under tremendous pressure. China has to change its development model to one that is more driven by domestic consumption and internal dynamics, in line with its vast geographical size and huge regional potential. Such a model helps lay the foundation for China to achieve economic restructuring and sustained national growth in the coming years.[1]

State Efforts to Address Regional Economic Disparity

Widening regional inequality is one of the major obstacles to achieving sustainable domestic economic development. Various constraints have held back development of the vast inland central and western regions, resulting in lack of economic competitiveness. The severe regional inequality not only inhibits sustainable development in China but also poses serious challenges to national unity and social stability. As is

---

[1] Yu Hong, *Chinese Regions in Change: Industrial Upgrading and Regional Development Strategies,* London and New York, Routledge, 2015.

evident in Xinjiang, regional deprivation provides the breeding ground for social instability and separatist movements in China.

In contrast to the coastal eastern region, which enjoys favourable state policies that include the establishment of special economic zones and open cities, as well as preferential taxation treatment, the western region is lagging far behind. People in the western region are increasingly incensed and frustrated by the state's biased regional policy, perceiving it as unfair and unjustified. Provincial and metropolitan policymakers in the interior regions are therefore aggressively lobbying the central government to demand for standardisation of policy treatment across regions, including more state fiscal transfer payments and aid for their regions.

Although the inequality issue attracted considerable academic and policy research interest over the years, the central government only started to address the problem in 1999 with the enforcement of the "Great Western Development" strategy. This was followed by the "Plan for the Rise of the Central Region" in 2002 and the "Revitalization Plan for the Northeastern Region" in 2003. Measures include introducing more favourable policy initiatives and state aid for large-scale infrastructure projects and development of specialised local industries. The proposed policy initiatives are intended to promote an equitable and sustainable model of regional development, and mark a shift in China's regional policy towards the interior regions.

The central government has started to channel more capital investment to the underdeveloped interior regions. According to estimations by the National Development and Reform Commission, state investment in western development projects had risen to 5.6 trillion yuan since the launch of the "Great Western Development" strategy in 2000.[2] The lion's share of this investment were allocated to infrastructure improvement in the inland regions as the Chinese authority

---

[2] "2015nian xibu dakaifa xinkaigong 30xiang zhongdian gongcheng" (The Newly Constructed 30 Major Projects for Western Development in 2015) National Development and Reform Commission, at <http://xbkfs.ndrc.gov.cn/gzdt/201512/t20151223_768415.html> (accessed 14 May 2016).

believes that infrastructure development is the key to stimulating economic growth, in addition to reduced intra- and interregional transportation costs for goods and people in the remote central, western and north-eastern regions.

Along with infrastructure development, the central government recognises the vital role of interregional industrial transfer in enhancing industrial and economic competitiveness in the underdeveloped central and western regions. To promote transfer to the underdeveloped central and western regions, the central authority introduced an initiative to set up several national-level interregional industrial transfer parks. Under this initiative, the implementation of industrial upgrading and economic restructuring from a capital- and labour-driven to an innovation-driven growth model in the eastern region will also be applied in the inland regions.

The Chinese authority's efforts to achieve a more balanced regional economic development only began to pay off towards the end of the Hu Jintao–Wen Jiabao era. As shown in Table 1 and Figure 2, the coefficient of variation, which is a measure of regional economic inequality, has gradually narrowed since 2010.

Table 1:   Changes in Regional Composition of GDP, 2001–2014 (%)

Year	Eastern Region	Central Region	Western Region
2001	57.5	26.9	15.6
2002	59.0	25.4	15.6
2003	58.5	26.2	15.3
2004	58.4	26.4	15.2
2005	59.6	25.4	15.0
2006	59.7	25.3	15.0
2007	59.3	25.6	15.2
2008	58.4	26.2	15.4
2009	57.9	26.3	15.8

(*Continued*)

Table 1: (*Continued*)

Year	Eastern Region	Central Region	Western Region
2010	60.7	25.7	13.6
2011	60.0	26.0	14.0
2012	59.5	26.5	14.0
2013	59.3	26.4	14.3
2014	58.9	26.3	14.8

Source: Compiled by the author based on National Bureau of Statistics, *China Statistical Yearbook*, China Statistics Press, various years.

Xi Jinping's Vision for Coordinated Regional Development

Common prosperity is essential to both retaining the performative legitimacy of the Chinese Community Party (CCP) and maintaining sustainable national economic development. Chinese President Xi Jinping, who is also general secretary of the CCP, has reiterated the significance of a balanced regional development and equitable prosperity in China. As the previous administration failed to find an effective solution to tackle regional economic disparity, Xi and other new Chinese leaders are determined to rise to the challenge. As reflected in his collection of speeches and writings in his book titled *The Governance of China*,[3] Xi had already formulated his grand vision and long-term strategy for China's development before he became the president of China in 2012. Furthermore, Xi was well prepared for the top leadership post even before being elected as the general secretary of the CCP under China's meritocracy.

Before taking over the helm from Hu Jintao, Xi had many years of work experience at various levels of local and central governments, ranging from Zhengding county in Hebei province, Ningde and Xiamen city in Fujian to Zhejiang province and Shanghai. Xi therefore has first-hand knowledge of the disparity in regional development, and

---

[3]Xi Jinping, *The Governance of China*, Beijing, Foreign Languages Press, 2014.

understands the local development issues faced by China. Xi's wealth of experience has guided him in formulating his vision on China's regional development when he became the president.

Xi has promulgated two main plans, namely the "Third Plenum Decision of the Chinese Communist Party on Comprehensive Reform" issued in 2013 and the "13th Five-Year Plan for National Socio-economic Development (2016–2020)" announced in 2016. These plans reflect the major commitment of current Chinese leaders to pursue spatial economic egalitarianism and regional equality as prerequisites of social justice and equality. Xi's vision for China is conceptualised in his "China Dream" — i.e. making the country stronger through development and reform, and achieving major national rejuvenation. Coordinated and balanced regional development — an important element in the "China Dream" discourse — has thus become a permanent fixture in state discourse and key development goal under Xi.

Xi's promise in his own words that "no region should be left behind for development", "common prosperity for all regions" and "revitalisation of the north-east region" underline his belief that achieving sustainable national development and social justice is premised on spatial socio-economic egalitarianism. In comparison with the "Three Represents" and "Scientific Outlook on Development" theoretical slogans advocated by Xi's predecessors, Jiang Zemin and Hu Jintao, respectively, Xi's doctrine and strategy for domestic regional development is perceived to be more solid, practical and straightforward.

The central government had successively formulated a series of bold regional development policy initiatives over the past three years, incorporating them in the "13th Five-Year Plan", the guiding plan for 2016 to 2020. For the first time since the Deng era, the slogan "common prosperity" has been formally adopted as China's key policy objective.

To achieve the goal of national rejuvenation in realising the "China Dream", the Xi Jinping–Li Keqiang administration formulated several important initiatives over the past three years, including the "One Belt, One Road" (OBOR) initiative, "Plan for Revitalisation of the North-eastern Region", "Plan for Development of Yangtze River Economic Belt" and "Plan for Coordination Development for the Beijing–Tianjin–Hebei Economic Zone". In Xi's view, these state-driven regional development plans help improve intraregional and inter-regional physical connectivity that involves infrastructure construction, address problems of fragmented regional markets and regional protection, and forge a unified and efficient national market based on free flow of resources, capital and people.

The Chinese Government's Agenda under Xi

Xi, similar to his predecessors, has to find ways to guide the national discourse to ensure socialism stay relevant and remain enshrined in the country in the face of a fast-changing internal environment and trans-forming external dynamics of the outside world. Xi highlights in his rhetoric socialism with Chinese characteristics, social equality, the role of a strong state and state intervention, and his vision of deepening compre-hensive reforms of the social, economic, political, propaganda, education and Party-building systems, all of which can be collectively referred to as neosocialism. Neosocialism has been implicitly incorporated into the prevailing "China Dream" discourse advocated by the Party–state.

To eliminate potential opposition to the reforms from various vested interests, Xi has centralised his power and established new top-level organisations — the Central Small Leading Group to Deepen Comprehensive Reform and the National Security Council — installing himself as chair. Xi also has direct oversight of the regional development coordination of the Beijing–Tianjin–Hebei Economic Zone, the Yangtze River Economic Belt and the north-eastern region. Leveraging the implementation of the OBOR initiative, Xi is deter-mined to achieve breakthrough in coordinating the regional develop-ment of the three said regions in the coming years.[4] He vouched for this in his speech at the Fifth Plenum of the 18th Party Congress.

As the lack of vibrant megacity clusters in China's vast interior regions is a major attributing factor to economic underdevelopment of the inland regions, the new Five-Year Development Plan proposes the

---

[4]"Xi Jinping's Speech at the Fifth Plenum of CCP's 18th Congress", 29 October 2015, at <http://cpc.people.com.cn/n1/2016/0104/c64094-28009486.html> (accessed 13 May 2016).

development of new city-clusters and mega metropolitan regions in the central, western and north-eastern regions to accelerate urbanisation, stimulate economic development and strengthen local competitiveness. The Beibu Gulf Economic Zone, Chengdu–Chongqing cluster and Lanzhou–Xining are examples of city-clusters highlighted in the state's plan.

To further boost economic growth, the Chinese government has invested heavily in transport and other infrastructure improvement in these regions to better interregional physical connectivity. In 2015, China pumped in 768.6 billion yuan in large-scale western development projects, including railway construction, expressways, airports, energy, power stations and other infrastructure facilities. The Guiyang–Kunming and Chongqing–Wanzhou high-speed railways are expected to be operational by the end of 2016, and China has further plans to build Guiyang–Nanning, Chongqing–Kunming and Xining–Chengdu high-speed railways.[5]

By increasing the capital pool that funds western development projects, particularly infrastructure projects that link China's border regions with neighbouring countries, the Chinese government plans to leverage financial resources from the Silk Road Fund, the newly established Asian Infrastructure Investment Bank as well as other multilateral development institutions to co-finance these large-scale cross-border infrastructure projects.

In order to draw on foreign expertise and experience in promoting regional development, a third government-to-government development project between Singapore and China was launched in Chongqing, an emerging city in western China. This project is identified as the keystone of China's ambitious OBOR initiative and its western regional development strategy.[6] Chongqing will become not

---

[5]National Development and Reform Commission, "2016 nian shenru tuijin xibu dakaifa gongzuo yaodian" (Major Tasks for Pushing Western Development in 2016), at <http://www.sdpc.gov.cn/gzdt/201605/t20160505_800984.html> (accessed 7 December 2016).

[6]"Singapore and China Hold 'Candid and In-Depth' Discussions during Xi Jinping's Visit", *The Strait Times*, 7 November 2015, at <http://www.straitstimes.com/singapore/

only the operational base for interregional physical connectivity in the western region, but also an important transportation and operation pivot for China–Europe freight trains, thereby leading to the opening up of western China.

Using the existing international cooperation platforms and regional coordination mechanisms under the OBOR framework as leverage, the Chinese government is keen to encourage further opening-up and advance local economic development of the underdeveloped regions in western China. Specifically, China plans to develop gateways or corridors to connect its western areas that border with neighbouring Asian countries and to transform places such as Xinjiang, Yunnan, Guangxi, Heilongjiang, Jilin and Inner Mongolia into regional hubs of transportation, trade and logistics.[7]

By advancing the OBOR initiative through the Beibu Gulf Economic Zone and Greater Pearl River Delta Economic Zone, the Chinese authority hopes to strengthen interaction and cooperation among the developed eastern region and the underdeveloped central and western regions. Since Xi took office in 2012, various implementations to reduce regional economic disparity gained momentum (Figure 2). The improved economic performance and competitiveness of central and western regions are evidence of strong state support.

Challenges in the Pursuit of Coordinated Regional Development

China has witnessed narrowing regional disparity at modest rate in recent years. The economies of underdeveloped inland regions are,

---

singapore-and-china-hold-candid-and-in-depth-discussions-during-xi-jinpings-visit> (accessed 20 May 2016).

[7]"Vision and Actions on Jointly Building Silk Road Economic Belt and 21st-Century Maritime Silk Road", jointly issued by China's National Development and Reform Commission, Ministry of Foreign Affairs and Ministry of Commerce, March 2015, at <http://xbkfs.ndrc.gov.cn/qyzc/201503/t20150330_669366.html> (accessed 20 May 2016).

however, still weak and vulnerable because the government, rather than the market, plays the dominant role in boosting regional economic and industrial growth. These regions have yet to develop a sustainable development model that is supposed to thrive on a vibrant private sector and competitive entrepreneurship. Both domestic and foreign investors therefore lack the incentives to invest in large-scale manufacturing and service projects in the western and north-eastern regions, certainly not at the scale that they had invested in the eastern regions.

Achieving sustainable and coordinated regional development in China is hence one of the major challenges to Xi's neosocialist style of government. Despite much fanfare from the media and officials, the government's efforts to address regional economic disparities have so far borne little fruits. The disparity in GDP per capita between the eastern region and the central and western regions continues to increase.

One of the pressing issues that Xi faced is inaction in the bureaucratic system and local bureaucracy due to power centralisation and the ongoing high-profile anti-graft campaign against corrupt officials. The central government is reliant on local governments for implementation of policy initiatives for the regions. Therefore, unless the central government can motivate local officials to perform their roles effectively, achieving balanced regional development will be an uphill task.

Another pressing issue that the interior regions face is their vulnerable ecological system and poor environmental conditions. Compared to the previous administration, the current government's regional development policy has given greater weight to environmental issues. As outlined in the 13th Five-Year Plan (2016–2020),[8] the Chinese government will adopt a new concept of regional development that introduces four types of functional zoning, namely optimised development zone, prioritised development zone, restricted development zone

---

[8] "The 13th Five-Year Plan for National Socio-economic Development (2016–2020)", approved by China's National People's Congress in March 2016, at <http://news.xinhuanet.com/politics/2016lh/2016-03/17/c_1118366322_21.htm> (accessed 15 May 2016).

and prohibited development zone based on the carrying capacity of the local ecological system and environment, the density of current development, resource endowment and the development potential of locality.[9] As the western region is the most ecologically sensitive and environmentally fragile part of China, there is inevitably a trade-off between boosting western economic development and protecting the local environment by restricting industrial activities, and this essentially poses a policy dilemma for the Chinese government.

The rugged and mountainous terrain of much of the central and western regions poses accessibility challenges and puts a strain on developing transportation. The authority refers to these areas as concentrated contiguous poor areas with special difficulties (*jizhong lianpian tesu kunan diqu*). The sheer size of these regions spatially but with deficiencies of transport system is appalling. While the central government has promised to substantially increase investment in transport and other infrastructure projects to improve intraregional and interregional connectivity for the concentrated contiguous poor areas with special difficulties and other economically poor areas in central and western regions from 2016 to 2020,[10] it may take many years down the road to develop a comprehensive transport network comprising high-speed railways, airports, power plants and expressways.

---

[9] An optimised development zone refers to a region with high density land development and a declining carrying capacity of resources and environment; a prioritised development zone refers to a region with strong resource endowment and environmental carrying capacity; a restricted development zone refers to a region with weak resource endowment and environmental carrying capacity, and plays a crucial role in national ecological security and food safety; and a prohibited development zone refers to legally established natural and cultural reserves in which industrial activities are prohibited.

[10] "Zhonggong zhongyang guowuyuan guanyu daying tuopin gongjianzhan de jueding" (Decision on Winning the Fight on Anti-Poverty by the Central Committee of Chinese Communist Party and State Council of China), The State Council Leading Group Office of Poverty Alleviation and Development, 29 November 2015, at <http://www.cpad.gov.cn/art/2015/12/7/art_46_42386.html> (accessed 15 May 2016).

In the first quarter of 2016, Liaoning, Jilin and Heilongjiang — the three north-eastern provinces — were among the poorest performing provinces in China in terms of economic growth, with Liaoning recording negative growth for the first time since 1978. In fact, since 2013, economic growth in the north-eastern region has slowed sharply, and the region's average growth rate compares poorly against the national average (Figure 3). The decline in north-eastern China's economic importance to the nation is reflected in a downward trend, from 10.87% in 1999 to 8.7% in 2015, and this has further aggravated since 2012 (Figure 4). However, in the context of China's economy adjusting to the "new normal", such a downturn is quite alarming to scholars of regional economy.

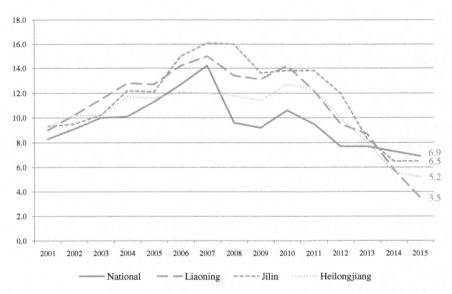

Figure 3: Comparison of GDP Economic Growth between the North-eastern Regions and the Nation as a Whole, 2001–2015 (%)

Sources: National Bureau of Statistics of China, *China Statistical Yearbook 2015*, China Statistics Press; Liaoning Provincial Bureau of Statistics, *Liaoning Statistical Yearbook* 2015, China Statistics Press; *Heilongjiang Statistical Yearbook 2015*; *Public Report for National Socio-economic Development 2015*; *Public Report for Socio-economic Development in Liaoning 2015*; *Public Report for Socio-economic Development in Jiling 2015*; *Public Report for Socio-economic Development in Heilongjiang 2015*.

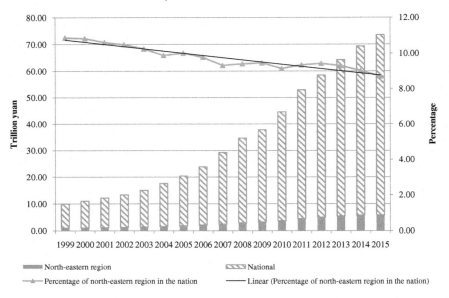

Figure 4: Contribution of North-eastern Provinces to China's GDP, 1999–2015

Sources: National Bureau of Statistics of China, *China Statistical Yearbook 2015*, China Statistics Press; Liaoning Provincial Bureau of Statistics, *Liaoning Statistical Yearbook* 2015, China Statistics Press; *Heilongjiang Statistical Yearbook 2015*; *Public Report for National Socio-economic Development 2015*; *Public Report for Socio-economic Development in Liaoning 2015*; *Public Report for Socio-economic Development in Jiling 2015*; *Public Report for Socio-economic Development in Heilongjiang 2015*.

Three major problems that affect the local economy of the north-eastern region are overdependence on resource-extraction industries and state capital investment, dominance of uncompetitive state-owned enterprises (SOEs), and underdevelopment of the service sector. For example, state capital investment accounted for over 65% of the north-eastern region's GDP in 2013. The north-eastern region's contribution of gross capital formation to GDP at 63.6%, which was substantially higher than the national average of 45.9%, underlines its heavy economic dependence on state investment.[11]

---

[11] National Bureau of Statistics of China, *China Statistical Yearbook 2015*, Beijing, China Statistics Press, 2015.

As China proceeds to restructure its economy from a capital-driven to an innovation-driven development model, the old model of dependency on state investment, SOE dominance and resource exploitation has gradually become outdated and unsustainable. Despite the implementation of the revitalisation plan in 2003, the north-eastern region has continued to adhere to the SOE-dominated and state-driven model. The north-eastern region lacks a genuinely competitive market or a prosperous private sector due to the overwhelming dominance of the state sector. The self-sustaining and spectacular economic performance that the eastern region has achieved is testament to the fact that a vibrant private sector and huge foreign investment are necessary ingredients to the success. The private sector lays the foundation for broad-based economic development, and provides impetus by bringing in physical capital, technology, competition culture and advanced management expertise.

It is a known major problem that the investment environment of the north-eastern region's economy is largely shaped by the local institutions and bureaucratic system, barring the fact that an efficient and transparent bureaucratic system is essential for economic growth in any regions or countries.[12] Rodrik, Subramanian and Trebbi's study[13] identifies quality of institutions as the universal and most important factor in boosting economic growth and determining income levels in regions and as instrumental to the development of commerce and manufacturing industries.

Over the last decade, the central government had implemented a series of preferential policy initiatives and development strategies, and provided massive amounts of state aid to the underdeveloped western and north-eastern regions. However, these regions have failed to develop a well-functioning institutional framework and an efficient

---

[12] Ash Amin, "An Institutionalist Perspective on Regional Development", *International Journal of Urban and Regional Research*, vol. 23, 1999, pp. 365–378.

[13] Dani Rodrik, Arvind Subramanian and Francesco Trebbi, "Institutions Rule: The Primacy of Institutions Over Geography and Integration in Economic Development", *Journal of Economic Growth*, vol. 9, 2004, pp. 131–165.

bureaucratic system that are vital to the development of a vibrant private sector.

Indeed, proactiveness from government bodies in promoting private business and creating a level playing field for state and non-state sectors is imperative in order to develop and nurture a pro-business and market-oriented investment environment. Domestic and foreign investors have long complained about the very high business transaction costs in the north-eastern region, mainly due to red tape and rigid bureaucracy inherited from the central planning economy back in the 1950s. Private investors are also currently less interested in investing in the north-eastern region compared to the eastern region due to the former's unfavourable institutional arrangements. The provincial and local governments of the north-eastern region should take a serious view of these complaints and improve the quality of institutional arrangements and efficiency of regulatory agents.

Widely perceived as being inefficient, inactive, unaccountable and corrupt, local officials in the north-eastern region have become a major target for China's ongoing high-profile anti-corruption campaign. This has resulted in the sacking and arrests of a number of high-ranking government and ministerial officials involved in corruption scandals over the last two years. It goes without saying that the anti-corruption drive has disruptive impact leading to inaction of local officials, and the low efficiency and poor capability of local institutions have also further exacerbated the situation of economic inactivity in the region.

Chapter 12

China's Population Policy and the Future of Its Labour Market

Jane DU*

Introduction

Labour, in addition to capital, is also a key element of a nation's economic growth. For China, the country with the largest population in the world, labour shortage has rarely been a problem. In fact, in response to the population boom in the 1950s, the Chinese government had experimented with various measures to control its population size since 1962 in order to maintain the per capita capital stock in steady state. The result was the implementation of the restrictive "one-child policy" in 1981.

However, in recent years, there have been calls for the government to relax population control as labour shortage looms large in China. First, total fertility rate declined sharply from 6.2 in 1962 to 1.7 in 2013 due to population control and economic development. Second, the elderly dependent ratio also rose considerably from 8.0 to 13.1 over the same period.[1] The Chinese government has shown a willingness to gradually relax population control. In 2013, China first relaxed its

* Jane DU is Visiting Research Fellow at the East Asian Institute, National University of Singapore.
[1] Total fertility rate is the average number of children that would be born per female if all females lived to the end of their childbearing years and bore children according

controversial one-child policy by allowing couples to have two children if one of the parents is an only child. At the end of 2015, the Chinese government removed this condition, making a two-child family a choice for all couples.

However, it seems the easing of the one-child policy has little effect on stimulating China's fertility rate. General fertility rate continues to dip after a short rebound in response to the population easing in 2013.[2] There are apparently other factors weighing in on a couple's fertility decision and China requires stronger efforts in policy implementation to liberalise population control. Despite the recent easing of the one-child policy, a United Nations (UN) population survey projects China's effective labour supply to shrink by 20% by 2050. Around a quarter billion of workers will quit China's labour market by then. Some scholars cautioned that the current policy easing is unlikely to reverse China's declining labour supply in the near future. Stronger efforts to boost population growth are required to deter the looming labour shortage.

Besides policy efforts, the timing of policy implementation also matters. In the past five decades, childbearing-age women decreased by an average of 14% every 10 years. Compared with the size of female population from the post-1970s generation, those from the post-1990s generation shrank by a quarter and those from the post-2000s generation dwindled by half. With a fast-decreasing population base of childbearing-age women, the cost of promoting population growth will continuously increase. In 10 years' time, the post-1970s and post-1980s generations will lose their reproductive window and be replaced

---

to the age-specific fertility rates for that area and period. This distinguishes it from the general fertility rate.

[2] General fertility rate is the total number of live births per 1,000 women of childbearing age in a population per year. This is a more refined way to measure fertility in a population than birth rate and total fertility rate because the general fertility rate accounts for the female population aged 15 to 44 years in the denominator, rather than the whole population. The general fertility rate reflects the potential fertility behaviour only and takes age distribution into account. This distinguishes from the total fertility rate. See footnote 1.

by the post-1990s and post-2000s generations in population reproduction. Hence, if policies to boost population growth are not implemented instantly, any measures could hardly reverse the imminent plummet in labour supply given the smaller female population base. In short, the Chinese government's hesitancy in taking advantage of the population size of the post-1970s and post-1980s generation implies that the effectiveness of population enhancement policies will be curtailed.

Demographic change is a chronic issue. Population policies take at least 20 years to have an effect on socio-economic development. Such long-term effect of population change may not be apparent in the short term, but has sufficient impact to handle an unavoidable blow to the nation. The Chinese government is aware of the impending population problems as evident by the implementation of the two-child policy at the end of 2015. However, the government's move to relax population control is not adequate in today's context and it is imperative that swift and stronger policy efforts are made.

China's Evolving Population Policies

Economic development relies on two basic elements, namely capital and labour. With significant changes in capital stock sorely lacking, labour becomes the only way to control and balance stagnating capital accumulation. Population policies are essentially used by modern states to alleviate resource scarcity by adjusting existing per capita resource possession through population control. If economic growth is hampered due to a lack of resource, states are inclined to adopt interventional policies to control their population. Populous countries such as China tend to gravitate towards such a move.

China's conscientious efforts in population control first came about in 1962 to address the rapid population boom in the 1950s during Mao Zedong's rule as he promulgated that "of all things, people are the most precious in the world". In the face of economic stagnation, China's economic backwardness was largely attributed to its large population. Before the Chinese economy opened up in the 1980s,

China's three major phases of negative economic growth signalling the economy's path of descent — namely the Great Famine, and the early and later stages of the Cultural Revolution — had induced the government to gradually tighten population control.

The first phase of tightening came about in the early 1960s when per capita gross domestic product (GDP) declined by more than 20% during the 1960–1962 period (Table 1). After the second phase of descent in 1966–1968, family planning was enhanced with a formal endorsement in the State Council Document No. 51 (1971). As China faced the near collapse of its economy on the eve of the reform, a set of new restrictive birth controls was implemented towards the end of the 1970s — "family planning" was written into the 1978 People's Republic of China Constitution with a stringent enforcement of the "one-child policy" in the 1981 Marriage Law (Table 1).

As the one-child policy was enacted at the same time as China started its economic reform leading to the take-off of the economy,

Table 1:   Major Population Policies in China, 1962–1981

Year	Change in Per Capita GDP	Keywords	Formal Endorsement
1960–1962	−20.62%	Instructions on birth control	The Chinese Communist Party Document No. 698. "Instruction on Earnestly Advocating Family Planning", 18 December 1962.
1966–1968	−12.60%	To enhance the family-planning work	The State Council Document No. 51. "The Report of Making a Good Job of Family Planning", 8 July 1971.
1975–1976	−3.36%	Family planning and one-child policy	The People's Republic of China (PRC) Constitution (1978), Article 53. "The state advocates and promotes family planning" and the PRC Marriage Law (1981), Articles 2 and 12 are for "one-child policy".

Sources: Compiled by the author from various sources of information, including the National Bureau of Statistics of China.

many attributed China's rapid social development to this policy. The one-child policy was also deemed to have produced a privileged, well-educated generation, the post-1980s, unprecedented in Chinese history. This development is especially good for economic growth in the 2000s and 2010s when the first one-child generation becomes the pillar of the whole nation.

However, from birth to entering the labour force, it will take individuals in the population at least 18 years to do so, and then another four decades to reach retirement. In other words, an individual takes 18 to 60 years to become fully involved in the economic circle. It is noteworthy that there is a huge time lag for a population policy to have an impact on the economy.

The Looming Labour Shortage

China's recent economic growth has benefited from the high total fertility rate in the 1960s and 1970s (Figure 1), as well as the restrictive policies since the 1980s. Fertility restriction implemented since the 1980s has reduced child dependency pressure in the short term and allowed the government to divert social resources to production. The outcome of such an enhancement to economic growth is however very limited and likely to have short-term effects. The move to reduce total fertility rate from record highs in the 1960s to below the replacement level in the 2010s is equivalent to continuously releasing labour supply that was saved before the 1970s,[3] without subsequent labour accumulation which is imperative. This development had steadily powered the post-reform boom given the sufficient labour supply from people born in the 1960s and 1970s. However, the fast-decreasing total fertility rate implies a serious labour shortage in China's future labour market which will be at the expense of future growth.

In less than five years, by 2020, people born in the 1960s will be in their 60s and gradually entering retirement age. When age groups with

---

[3] China's total fertility rate in 2013 was 1.66, a sharp drop an all-time high of 6.2 in 1962.

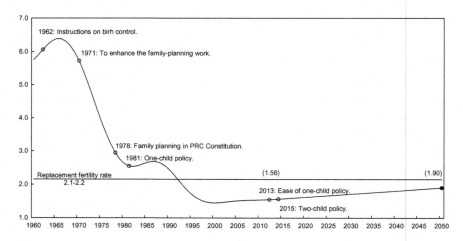

Figure 1: Total Fertility Rate in China, 1960–2050

Notes: [a]Replacement level fertility is the reproduction level of a woman in replacing herself and her mate.

[b]According to the United Nations (UN) survey, China's total fertility rate in 2050 is approximated to be 1.90.

Sources: World Bank, World DataBank, at <http://databank.worldbank.org/data/home.aspx> (accessed 20 May 2015); United Nations, "World Population Ageing, 1950–2050", at <http://www.un.org/esa/population/publications> (accessed 20 May 2015).

large population base begin to retire, the drastic drop in total fertility rate during the 1960–1980 period will further exacerbate the situation of effective labour supply in China. The labour supply appears to face imminent shortage. The dependency ratio reported in 2013 sample population survey is 46%,[4] which means there are 46 elderly and youths for every 100 working-age people to take care of. The dependency ratio will increase to 64% in 2050, implying that 39% of the Chinese population need care.[5] The size of working-age popula-

---

[4]Dependency ratio includes both elderly and child dependency ratios.

[5]Meanwhile, according to a UN survey on world population, by 2050, the older Chinese population aged 60 and above would reach 437 million, accounting for 29.89% of the total population of 1.46 billion; see United Nations, *World Population Ageing, 1950–2050*, at <http://www.un.org/esa/population> (accessed 20 May 2015).

tion will determine the future economic status of a nation. With sufficient capital accumulation, labour supply will be the backbone of China's future economic growth and determine the prospects of the Chinese economy. China's total fertility rate has fallen to below the replacement level for more than 20 years. A comparison based on replacement-level fertility at 2.2[6] estimates a 25% shrinkage in population for every next generation and a corresponding 25% shrinkage in labour supply in 18 years' time. The one-child policy has reduced the annual newly added labour supply from 3% in 1980 to 1% in 2015. The rate is set to halve and decline further to less than 0.5% in 2030. As a result, by 2050, effective labour supply is expected to shrink by 20% or a quarter billion workers in China's labour market.

The size of labour supply, as well as the structure, indeed matters to human capital accumulation, which also faces similar challenges. The expansion of higher education in 1999 has helped to accumulate human capital in China. However, as the share of working-age population with tertiary education increases, the problem of labour shortage (for the less educated ones) worsens. China's labour shortage is now looming large. A shrinkage of a small proportion of a quarter billion workers from the labour market would be considered labour decay, which will have unprecedented impact in history. Working-age population play an important role in generating consumption demand, and shaping the social structure and size of the economy. The larger the working-age population, the greater will be the effective domestic consumption and the potential for growth and development. A 20% shrinkage of the working-age population in China will thus reduce domestic consumption and generate fewer employment opportunities.

---

[6]In developed countries, replacement fertility rate is approximately 2.1 children per woman to maintain current population and demographic structure due to the preference for boy newborns and the higher-than-average infant mortality rate of girls all over the world. Taking into account the higher infant mortality rate, replacement-level fertility in developing countries is slightly higher than the world average. Hence, replacement-level fertility at 2.2 is widely accepted in academia.

As consumption decreases with declining labour supply, this dual shrinkage will eventually cause a downturn in China's economy size.

The 2015 Two-Child Policy: Too Weak and Too Late?

Although the government abolished the one-child policy in 2015/2016 to allow all families to have two children, the move is insufficient to reverse the trend of a sharp decline in China's labour supply. After 34 years of fertility restriction, having only one child has become the social norm in China. While the two-child policy did open the door for Chinese families to have more than one child, the government's long-time fertility restriction and rapidly rising costs of living weigh in on people's decision to have one more child. Despite a quick rebound in general fertility rate during the 2012–2013 period, it slid as rapidly as it had surged thereafter. The dip indicates that the effect of the relaxation of the one-child policy is very limited and the demographic trend in China is not expected to reverse immediately. Even if the general fertility rate has been successfully raised, it would take almost 20 years for the two-child policy to have an impact on the country's dependency ratios and labour supply.

According to a recent UN research on population dynamics change, it is projected that China's demographic change would worsen with potential support ratio plummeting from 12.8 in 1975 to 2.7 by 2050. Table 2 highlights some of the important indicators of structural change in China's demographic trend from 1975 to 2050. According to the World Bank data set and United Nations projection, the elderly population (65 years old and above) is estimated to soar from 110 million in 2010 to 470 million in 2050, accounting for a quarter of the total population. As is shown in Table 2, the share of working-age population (aged 15 to 59), will drop considerably from 65% in 2000 to 62.1% in 2025. From 2010 to 2050, China's labour force is expected to reduce by 250 million and the overall size of effective labour supply will shrink and return to the 1975 level.

The labour shrinkage in the context of a fourfold increase in elderly population seems especially significant. The potential support ratio

Table 2:   China's Population Forecast, 1975–2050

Indicator	1975	2000	2025	2050
Population (1,000 persons)	927,807.6	1,275,132.9	1,470,786.8	1,462,058.2
Total fertility rate (per woman)	3.3	1.8	1.9	1.9
Percentage in older ages (60+)	6.9	10.1	19.5	29.9
Percentage in 15–59 age group	*53.6*	*65*	*62.1*	*53.8*
Median age (years)	20.6	30.0	39.0	43.8
Dependency ratio (per cent)	78.2	46.4	46.2	63.9
Potential support ratio	12.8	10.0	5.2	2.7

Notes: Potential support ratio describes the burden of non-working elderly population on the working population aged between 15 and 64.
Source: United Nations, "World Population Ageing, 1950–2050", at <http://www.un.org/esa/population/publications> (accessed 20 May 2015).

(Table 2) reflects that by 2050, every elderly person in China will be paid and supported by only 2.7 working-age people, not taking into account the number of children under the care of the working-age group. This is aggravated by enhanced life expectancy and increased average wage level, thanks to the rapid economic growth for over 30 years. China's monetary support ratio as rendered by the working-age population would be significantly worse off, implying that the working-age generation will have to contribute more to social welfare.

Some Chinese population experts estimated the number of neonates following the relaxation of the one-child policy would add modest growth — about one to two million births — from 2013 to 2016; this estimation is now deemed too optimistic. The easing of the one-child policy in 2013 has yet to achieve its expected effect, not to mention narrow the gap between future labour demand and supply. From 2025 to 2050, the workforce in China is expected to decrease by 11.3%,[7] an unprecedented working-age population decline in human history.[8] This is in line with the current declining trend in the working-age population and the birth rate. The relaxation of the one-child policy is thus inadequate to alleviate China's labour market pressure.

Although initiating the two-child policy is a significant step forward, much more still needs to be done. The Chinese government needs to intensively launch promotional policies that boost fertility in order to arrest the workforce decline.

The Timing of the Intensive Promotional Population Policies

In addition to the long time lag for population policies to take effect, policy effectiveness also depends on the structure of the female population in the country. If there is rapid change to the structure of childbearing-age women, the timing of population policy implementation will significantly impact on the implementation cost and effectiveness. Table 3 and Figure 3 show the structure of China's current female population and the variations in fertility behaviour among different age groups.

In general, the number of childbearing-age women decreases by an average of 14% every 10 years. The post-1980s female population shrinks by 13% compared with that of the post-1970s; the post-2000s (children of post-1970s and 1980s) decreases even more — by a quarter — than that of the post-1990s. Over the past 10 years, the overall fertility behaviour of all female age groups has declined in China. Although women's fertility rate increased from 2011 to 2012,

---

[7] According to a UN survey on world population, the 15–64 working-age population in China would decrease from 1,006.1 million in 2025 to 892.0 million in 2050.

[8] From 1990 to 2013, the decline in Russia's working-age population, which underwent the fastest decline in modern history or otherwise known as depopulation bomb, was only 10.2%.

Table 3: Distribution of Fertile Women in China by Age Groups, 2013

Year of Birth	Sample Size (persons)[a]	Proportion (per cent)[b]	Estimate for Group Population (million persons)[c]	Decade-on-Decade Change Rate (per cent)
1960–1964	46,719	8.15%	52.83	post–1960s
1965–1969	56,494	9.86%	63.88	—
1970–1974	53,461	9.33%	60.45	post–1970s
1975–1979	39,901	6.96%	45.12	−9.54%
1980–1984	37,803	6.60%	42.74	post–1980s
1985–1989	43,636	7.61%	49.34	−12.77%
1990–1994	39,345	6.87%	44.49	post–1990s
1995–1999	33,610	5.86%	38.00	−10.42%
2000–2004	28,296	4.94%	31.99	post–2000s
2005–2009	27,018	4.71%	30.55	−24.18%

Notes: [a,b]Data of "sample size" and "proportion" in columns 2 and 3 were collected from the 2009 National Bureau of Statistics' survey of population.
[c]Female population in different age groups is estimated from the proportion in column 3 and the 2013 female population data.
Source: National Bureau of Statistics of China, National Data, at <http://data.stats.gov.cn/english/> (accessed 20 May 2015).

the fertility of women 20–24 and 25–29 age groups quickly fall again shortly thereafter.

This indicates that the easing of the one-child policy has little effect on female population in the 20–24 and 25–29 age groups. Interestingly, women in the 30–34 and 35–39 age groups registered positive, albeit slightly, response to the policy easing (Figure 2). The trend shows that easing the restrictive one-child policy has made a greater impact on the post-1970s and 1980s generations. In general, the trend in China conforms with the global trend of decreasing fertility rate along with economic growth. Sharp increase in China's youth dependency has

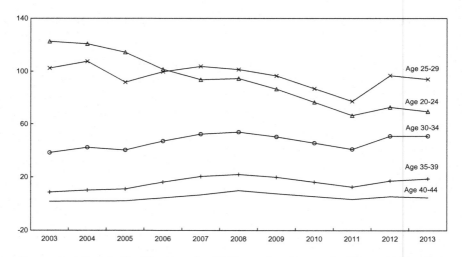

Figure 2: Female Fertility Rate for Different Age Groups in China, 2003–2013

Notes: Data for 2005 were estimates from the national 1% population sample survey. Data for other years were 1‰ (per mille) from national sample survey on population change. As the five-year National Population Census was taken in 2010, sample data survey for 2010 is not available.

Source: National Bureau of Statistics of China, National Data, at <http://data.stats.gov.cn/english/> (accessed 20 May 2015).

added pressure on the fertility decision-making of the 20–24 and 25–29 age groups.

Currently, China's growth in birth rate is mainly contributed by women born during the 1980–1995 period (Figure 3). Despite its lower fertility rate, contribution by the post-1970s generation is still significant given the much larger population base from this generation compared to the other generations. In 10 years' time, the post-1990s and post-2000s will replace the post-1970s and post-1980s as the biggest contributors to China's population growth. The cost of encouragement population policies will be significantly higher than current costs as the post-1970s and post-1980s women, with large population bases, will lose their fertility. Even if population-enhancing policies are implemented in succession for the post-1990s and post-2000s generations, the smaller population bases of females (of child-bearing age) from the said generations could barely reverse

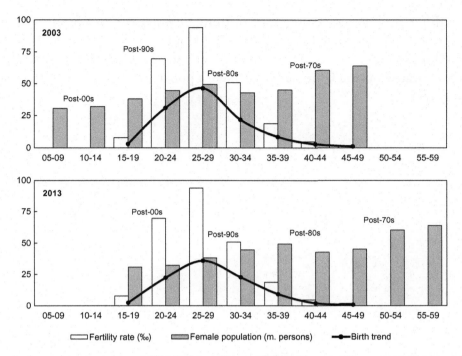

Figure 3: Estimates of the Effect of Two-Child Policy in China, 2003–2013

Source: National Bureau of Statistics of China, National Data, at <http://data.stats.gov.cn/english/> (accessed 20 May 2015).

the expected dive in labour supply. Thus, China cannot afford to miss the opportunity of capitalising on the population size of the post-1970s and post-1980s generations.

There is a chronic need to address demographic changes. Population policies will take a long time to take effect and contribute to socio-economic development. The population pool born half a century ago in the 1960s, or the post-1960s generation, have made a direct impact in achieving China's current economic status. The long-term effects of changes in population policy are not evident in the short term, but the impact will be wide-ranging and inevitable. China's ongoing labour shrinkage will render social resources less effective. The decline in labour supply may cause rapid outflow of resources and produce a growth pattern that is constrained by labour input. The future of China's labour market and economic growth pattern is thus largely predicated on the Chinese government's policies to boost population growth.

Chapter 13

Population Ageing and
Youth Drain — Impact on Growth

LU Ding*

For over three decades from the late 1970s to the first decade of this century, the Chinese economy grew at rates close to 10% per annum. This period of hyper economic growth coincided with an auspicious demographic transition, which provided huge comparative advantages for the country to industrialise with labour-intensive manufacturing.

Recent statistics suggest that China's demographic transition has passed a turning point where the previous demographic bonus is turning into an onus. Working-age population has embarked on a long-term declining trend and the nation is ageing quickly. "Youth drain", a particular pattern of migration by rural workers, exacerbates interregional disparity of development. All of these pose serious challenges to China's social and economic development in the coming years. This chapter reviews the key issues of the demographic challenges.

Demography: From Bonus to Onus

China's demographic transition since the founding of the People's Republic has experienced the following phases (Figure 1). In the

---

*LU Ding is Professor of Economics at the University of the Fraser Valley, Canada. He was a Visiting Senior Research Fellow at the East Asian Institute, National University of Singapore.

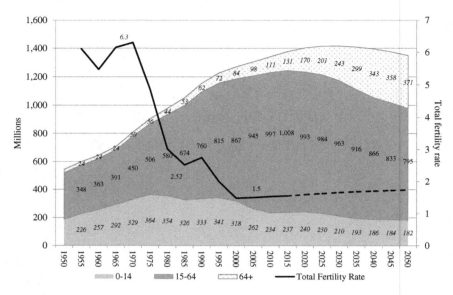

Figure 1: China's Population by Age Group and Total Fertility Rate

Source: United Nations, Department of Economic and Social Affairs, Population Division, *World Population Prospects: The 2015 Revision*, DVD Edition, 2015.

first phase from 1950 to 1975, when all the three age groups of the population — the child group (age 0–14), working-age group (age 15–64) and elderly group (age 65+) — expanded rapidly by numbers. Total population increased more than one third from 544 million in 1950 to 900 million in 1975. The baby boom from the 1950s to the 1960s enlarged the pool of children relative to the rest of the population, causing the total dependency ratio, namely, the number of dependents per 100 working-age persons, to reach a plateau in 1965–75.

The second phase started around 1975 when the number of child dependents (age 0–14) started to decline after reaching its peak of 364 million. This decline was a result of a sharp drop in total fertility rate, which fell from 6.3 children per woman in 1965–70 to 2.52 children per woman in 1980–85 and further dropped to 1.5 around 2005. Elsewhere in the world, rising standard of living typically leads to lower fertility rates thanks to growing opportunity costs of raising children for young couples. In China, however, the rapid fall in fertility rates was triggered and accelerated by the family planning programme launched by the government in the early 1970s, which advocated "later marriage, longer birth intervals and fewer births". After 1980 the family planning programme became more proactive and even compulsory with the introduction of the draconian one-child-per-couple policy.

Meanwhile, the baby-boom cohorts of child dependents in the previous phase were growing up and subsequently entering the working age, more than doubling the size of the working-age population from 450 million in 1970 to nearly one billion by 2010. Thanks to the combination of a bulging labour force and a shrinking pool of children to rear, the total dependency ratio kept falling for four decades from its plateau level, about 79 to 80 dependents per hundred working-age adults in 1965–1970, to a nadir of 34.5 dependents around 2010 (Figure 2).

This phase of demographic transition was extremely favourable to economic growth as it brought in huge "demographic dividends": The falling dependency ratio implied fewer young (and elderly) mouths to

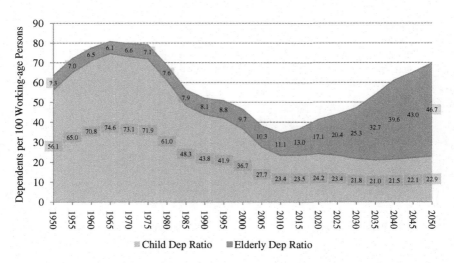

Figure 2:   China's Dependency Ratios

Source: United Nations, *World Population Prospects*.

feed and more youthful hands for hire. Per capita income growth was easier as long as most of those in working ages could find jobs. Meanwhile the bulging share of working-age adults in the population generated higher household savings that supported investment growth, intensifying capital use in production and thus enhancing labour productivity. These effects presented a huge "bonus" to economic growth.

As time passed, however, the shrinking pool of children resulted in fewer young adults entering the labour force in later years. The elderly cohorts of working-age population soon reached retirement age. With rising standard of living and improving health conditions, the elderly people live healthier and longer, putting an end to the expansion of working-age population and the decline in dependency ratio.

By around 2010, China's dependency ratio finally reached its nadir and started a long-term upward climb (Figure 2). Its working-age population also reached a turning point soon thereafter and is projected to fall continuously for decades to come. As shown in Figure 3, from its peak of 941 million in 2011, the size of the population aged 15–59

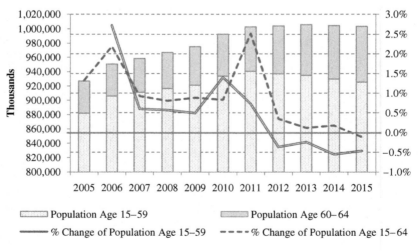

Figure 3: Working-Age Population (2005–2015)

Source: National Bureau of Statistics of China, <http://data.stats.gov.cn> (accessed 30 June 2016).

had declined accumulatively by nearly 2%. The size of population aged 15–64 also had started to shrink.

Hence the country has entered the third phase of demographic changes. Total population will reach its peak at about 1.4 billion around 2030 and start to shrink in decades afterwards. Most alarmingly, the population is ageing quickly: the elderly dependency ratio had already gone up from 7.6 in 1980 to 13.1 in 2015. It is projected to almost double by 2030 to 25.3 and continue to rise to near 46.7 by 2050.

The rising dependency ratios and a shrinking labour force are bound to have negative impact on household savings and per capita income growth, turning the demographic bonus to onus. The increasingly heavier burden of supporting a fast-growing elderly population and the tax base increasingly constrained by a shrinking labour force will work together to reduce social savings in coming years. Greater public spending on social security and health care to take care of the growing elderly population also means less public money available for investment in many physical infrastructure projects.

Passing the Lewis Turning Point

During the phase of demographic bonus, China's industrialisation had an additional boost from the abundant supply of rural surplus labour. It was observed by Lewis that the early stage of industrialisation in an economy dominated by traditional agricultural sector typically enjoys abundant labour supply at very low unit labour costs.[1] The continuous outflow of surplus labour from rural agriculture to urban industries keeps industrial wages from rising until industrialisation expands the modern industrial sector to the extent that all rural surplus labour is absorbed. Before passing that "Lewis turning point", industrialisation enjoys the benefit of low wages.

When China embarked on its market-oriented reform and modernisation programme three and a half decades ago, the country's level of

---

[1] W A Lewis, "Economic Development with Unlimited Supplies of Labor", *The Manchester School*, vol. 28, no. 2, 1954, pp. 139–191.

urbanisation was lagging behind its industrialisation. Around 1980, the primary sector (i.e. agriculture, including farming, forestry, animal husbandry and fishery) accounted for 70% of total employment but only produced about 30% of GDP. Meanwhile 81% of the population was rural residents. The great gap in labour productivity between the agricultural sector and other sectors indicated huge potential of surplus labour in the rural area.

China's rural labour started to move out of traditional agriculture when the rural township and village industries emerged in the 1970s. By the late 1970s and early 1980s, the post-Mao rural reform decollectivised agricultural production and restored it to household farming. The reform reinstilled incentives to farming and effectively raised agricultural productivity, resulting in the first wave of emigration of rural surplus labour to non-agricultural activities. Through the 1980s to the 1990s, however, the official urbanisation policy was the so-called "small town consensus" that encouraged *in situ* urbanisation by developing rural township and village enterprises. Migration of rural workers to large and medium-sized cities was strictly regulated by the *hukou* (household registration) system. Rural migrants who went to work and live in cities without official permit were frequently harassed by the police with arrests and forceful deportation.[2]

During those years, more and more people moved to work and live in places other than where their households were registered. Many of these migrants were not able to change the location of their household registration, thus constituting the population without *hukou* of residence and the so-called "floating population". There also emerged a new category of social class — the rural workers (*nongmin gong*, see Box 1 and Table 1).

The forceful deportation of rural migrants without permit lasted until 2003 when an important policy change abandoned the practice and allowed rural migrant workers to seek urban employment. That policy change removed a major barrier to rural-urban migration and enhanced the positive effect of such migration on economic growth,

---

[2]Lu Ding, "Policy Evolution of China's Regional Development", in *China's Evolving Industrial Policies and Economic Restructuring*, Zheng Yongnian and Sarah Tong, eds., Routledge, 2014, pp. 31–55.

Box 1: Definitions of Some Terms of Population Statistics

- Household-registered population (*huji renkou*) consists of persons residing at the place where their households are registered.
- Resident population (*changzhu renkou*) consists of persons residing in a household registered in a place for most time of the year or for more than six months.
- Urban population (*chengzhen renkou*) consists of persons residing in cities and towns for more than six months.
- Population without *hukou* of residence (*renhu fenli renkou*) consists of persons who reside in a place other than where their households are registered and have left their place of household registration for more than six months.
  - Floating population (*liudong renkou*) consists of persons without *hukou* of residence and residing beyond the city jurisdiction where their households are registered.
- Rural workers (*nongmin gong*) refers to persons with rural *hukou* but working in the non-agricultural sectors.
  - Local rural workers (*bendi nongmin gong*) are rural workers who work in non-agricultural sectors in the local rural areas where their households are registered.
  - Migrant rural workers (*waichu nongmin gong*) are rural workers who work in non-agricultural sectors in places other than the rural areas where their households are registered.

Table 1: China's Population Classifications

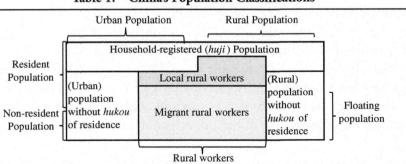

Source: Compiled from National Bureau of Statistics of China, Classifications and Methods, <http://www.stats.gov.cn> (accessed 15 July 2016).

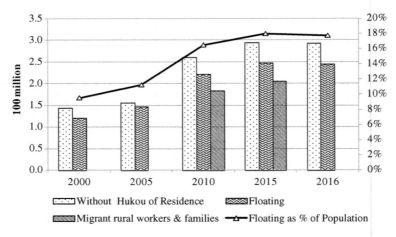

Figure 4:   Floating Population (2000–2015)

Note: Number of "migrant rural workers and families" is estimated by assuming that those migrant rural workers with family members have on average one dependent residing with the worker.

Source: National Bureau of Statistics of China, <http://www.stats.gov.cn> and <http://data. stats.gov.cn> (accessed 30 June 2016).

namely the "Kuznets effect", which typically occurs to a developing economy during industrialisation.[3]

When officially published results of annual surveys started to reveal statistics of floating population in 2000, its size already reached 121 million, or 9.5% of total population. In one and a half decades since then, the size has inflated to 247 million, accounting for 18% of population, signifying rising mobility of labour force (Figure 4).

Over 80% of the floating population consists of migrant rural workers and their families, as indicated by the official statistics of rural workers (*nongmin gong*) available since 2008 (Table 2). Migrant rural workers have been an indispensable part of the urban labour force. They take up over 40% of urban jobs and, with their family members, account for at least 26% of the urban population. Continuous flow of

---

[3] Simon Kuznets, "Quantitative Aspects of the Economic Growth of Nations II: Industrial Distribution of National Product and Labor Force", *Economic Development and Cultural Change*, vol. 5 no. 4, Supplement, 1957, pp. 3–110.

Table 2: Statistics of Rural Workers

	2008	2010	2011	2012	2013	2014	2015
Total number of rural workers (million persons), of which:	225.4	242.2	252.8	262.6	268.9	274.0	277.4
Migrant rural workers	140.4	153.4	158.63	163.4	166.1	168.2	168.8
- without family members	111.8	122.6	125.84	129.6	130.9	132.4	*132.9*
- with family members	28.6	30.7	32.79	33.8	35.3	35. 8	*35.9*
Local rural workers	85.0	88.9	94.15	99.3	102.8	105.7	108.6
Migrant rural workers as % of urban population*	27.1	27.5	27.7	27.7	27.5	27.2	26.6
% of urban jobs	43.7	44.2	44.2	44.0	43.4	42.8	41.8

*% of urban population is estimated by assuming that those migrant rural workers with family members have on average one dependent residing with the worker.
Sources: National Bureau of Statistics of China, <http://www.stats.gov.cn> and <http://data. stats.gov.cn> (accessed 30 June 2016).

migrant workers from rural areas to cities has provided abundant labour supply, the basis of China's comparative advantage in labour intensive manufacturing industries.

By official data, in 2015, primary sector accounted for 9% of GDP and 29% of total employment while 44% of population was residents in the rural area. Since the mid-1990s, China's urbanisation has been evolving rapidly, with about 20 million people being urbanised every year (Figure 5). Doubtlessly, this momentum will continue as per capita income rises. However, some of the statistical changes in urban population are the results of a redrawing of urban boundaries. According to survey data collected by researchers at the Southwest University of Economics and Finance, only about half of the urbanised population in the last 10 years were made up of rural-urban migrants.[4]

---

[4] "Gan Li: Economic Research in China is at the Primary Stage", *Caixin*, 4 July 2016, <http://finance.caixin.com/2016-07-04/100962156.html> (accessed 4 July 2016).

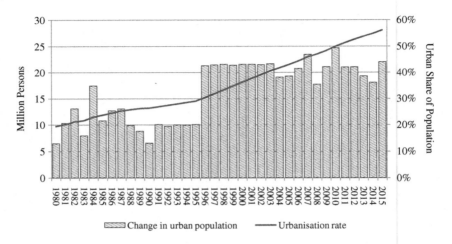

Figure 5: Change of Urban Population and Urbanisation Rate (1980–2015)
Source: National Bureau of Statistics of China, <http://www.stats.gov.cn> (accessed 30 June 2016).

The official statistics of rural workers based on annual surveys provide a picture closer to the reality of rural-urban migration. As shown in Figure 6, the annual growth rates of both all of rural workers and migrant workers have fallen drastically since 2010. Particularly, the growth of migrant rural workers almost came to a halt in 2015.

Was this fall in number of migrant rural workers due to weaker job market demand? In fact, according to the quarterly surveys on labour market in 101 cities (that account for 60% of urban population) by the Ministry of Human Resources and Social Security, the ratio of newly created positions to the number of jobseekers started at 0.65 in Q1 2001 and gradually rose over the years. It broke 1.0 threshold in Q1 2010 and reached the record high of 1.15 in Q4 2014. In other words, the ratio had been rising in most years since 2001 (when statistics became available) and had remained greater than one since 2010, indicating strong demand in the labour market (Figure 7).

Since the outflow of rural workers to the urban sector had been diminishing, the shortage of labour supply had resulted in a sharp rise in real wages. As shown in Figure 8, measured in real terms, both the urban minimum wage and urban average wage had been growing faster than non-agricultural labour productivity in recent years.

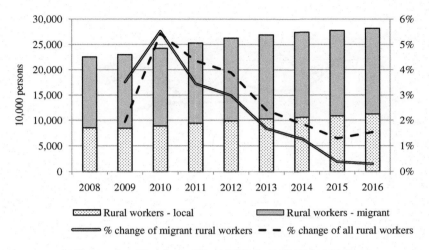

Figure 6: Number of Rural Workers (2008–2015)

Source: National Bureau of Statistics of China, <http://www.stats.gov.cn> (accessed 30 June 2016).

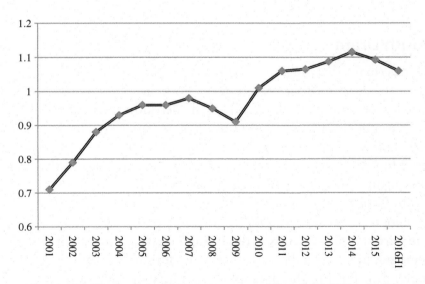

Figure 7: Newly Created Positions versus Jobseekers (2001–2016)

Source: Ministry of Human Resources and Social Security, <http://www.mohrss.gov.cn> (accessed 30 June 2016).

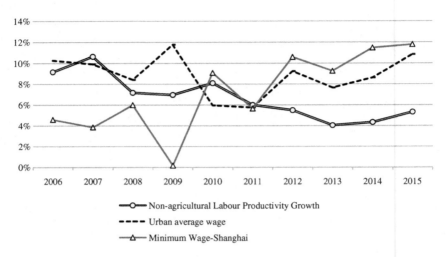

Figure 8: Wage Growth versus Labour Productivity Growth (2006–2015)

Source: National Bureau of Statistics of China, <http://www.stats.gov.cn> (accessed 30 June 2016) and Ministry of Human Resources and Social Security, <http://www.mohrss.gov.cn> (accessed 30 June 2016).

Youth Drain

China's rural-urban migration exhibits a particular pattern: The majority of the rural migrant workers who work and live in urban sectors have left behind their junior and elderly dependents in home villages. As shown in Table 2, only one in five migrant rural workers have taken their family members with them. Many of them plan to return and retire in their homeland after spending their prime years in the cities. This distinct phenomenon is called "youth drain".[5]

The "youth drain" pattern of migration is evident in the data of the fifth population census (2000) and the sixth population census (2010). The period 2000–2010 was the last decade that China enjoyed the demographic dividends embodied in a continuously falling dependency ratio. During the decade, the country's population increased

---

[5]Lu Ding, "'Youth Drain' and its Implication for Regional Disparity", *East Asian Policy*, vol. 6, no. 4, 2014, pp. 64–80.

5.84% from 1.267 billion to 1.341 billion. In comparison, its working-age population (15–64 years old) grew much faster by 14.1% from 869.81 million to 992.56 million. Consequently, nationwide total dependency ratio fell substantially from 42.86 to 34.28. Meanwhile, the population started to age quickly. The population median age rose almost eight years from 26.9 years old to 34.6 years old. While the child dependency ratio — the number of child dependents (aged 0–14 years) per 100 adults aged 15–64 years old — fell from 32.71 to 22.30, the elderly dependency ratio (number of those aged over 65 per 100 adults aged 15–64) rose from 10.15 to 11.98, signifying the beginning of an ageing society.

Between 2000 and 2010, due to the emigration of working-age population, China's rural area and poor regions saw their elderly dependency ratios (i.e. the ratio between those aged 65 years old and above and those aged 15–64 years old) as well as median population age rose faster than that in urban area and rich regions. These effects of "youth drain" are shown in Figure 9, which displays changes of dependency ratios in three categories of jurisdiction, namely cities, towns and rural (countryside), between the two census years. In the decade, child dependency ratios of all three categories fell while elderly dependency ratios rose. It is remarkable

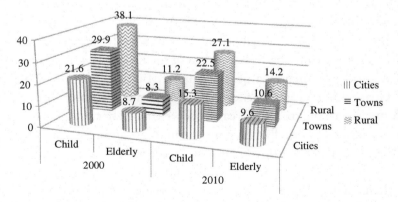

Figure 9: Dependency Ratios in Cities, Towns and Rural Areas (2000–2010)

Source: National Bureau of Statistics of China, Population Census data, <http://www.stats.gov.cn/tjsj/pcsj> (accessed 30 June 2016).

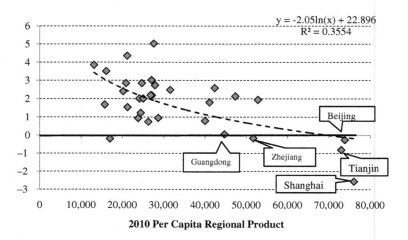

Figure 10: Changes in Elderly Dependency Ratios (2000–2010) versus Per Capita Regional Product (2010)

Source: National Bureau of Statistics of China, Population Census data, <http://www.stats.gov.cn/tjsj/pcsj> (accessed 30 June 2016).

that the elderly dependency ratio increased much faster in rural areas than in cities: In 2000, the rural elderly dependency ratio was 29% higher than the cities' but in 2010 it was 48% higher.

Cross-region changes in elderly dependency ratios also have uneven impacts that favour the rich regions. As shown in Figure 10, richer provinces experienced smaller increases in elderly dependency ratios while the poorer ones had greater rises in the ratios. The richest municipalities and provinces, namely Shanghai, Beijing, Tianjin, Zhejiang and Guangdong, even saw their elderly dependency ratios decline.

Similarly, in Figure 11, we can observe that richer provincial economies experienced smaller increase in median age of the population during the decade. Of the 31 provincial economies, 21 had per capita regional product of less than 32,000 yuan in 2010. Seventeen of the 21 saw their median age increased by five or more years in the decade and the average increase of median age of the 21 was 5.3 years. In contrast, of the 10 provincial economies with per capita income above 39,000 yuan, only three had their median age rise by more than five years. For the seven provinces with per capita income of above 39,000 yuan but

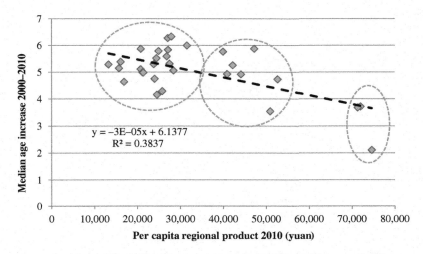

Figure 11: Changes in Median Age (2000–2010) versus Per Capita Regional Product (2010)

Source: Author's estimation from Population Census data, <http://www.stats.gov.cn/tjsj/pcsj> (accessed 30 June 2016).

below 70,000 yuan, their average increase of median age was five years. For the top three municipalities with per capita income exceeding 70,000 yuan, their median age increased on average by only 3.17 years.

"Youth drain" reallocates the working-age population between rural and urban areas, towns and cities, and poor regions and rich regions. By changing the demographic compositions across regions, the "youth drain" feature of migration moderates the negative impact of rising dependency ratios on per capita income growth at the receiving end of migration. As the country's demographic bonus turns into an onus, the "youth drain" exacerbates disparity of incomes between poor and rich areas. It is evident in Figure 12 that dependency ratios have a significantly negative correlation with per capita regional products across provincial economies. Over the decade of 2000–2010, the correlation became stronger (as shown in the increase of R-square values). The richer a provincial economy is, the smaller the dependency ratio.

There are two institutions that contribute to the "youth drain" phenomenon. One is the *hukou* (household registration) system and the other is the

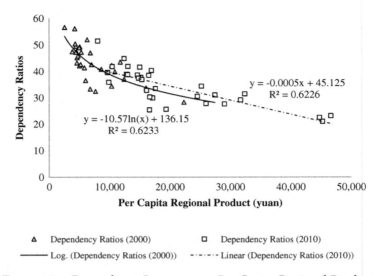

Figure 12: Dependency Ratios versus Per Capita Regional Products

Source: National Bureau of Statistics of China, Population Census data, <http://www.stats.gov. cn/tjsj/pcsj> (accessed 30 June 2016).

rural land tenure system. The former, introduced in the 1950s, divides the Chinese population into rural residents and urban residents whose *hukou* status was largely determined at birth and strictly regulated by local governments. Holding a local *hukou* status entitles the person to the locally provided public services. In the recent two decades, some reforms to household registration system have been introduced to accommodate labour mobility. Rural residents are now allowed to obtain *hukou* status in towns and small cities if they work and reside there on a prolonged basis. However, *hukou* status in large cities and metropolises is still largely inaccessible to rural migrant workers and their family members. Without the *hukou*-entitlement to crucial urban public services, it is very costly for migrant workers to bring their children or elderly parents to live in the cities. The lack of urban *hukou* has also condemned rural migrants to an underclass of marginally employable and disposable workers who face job discrimination and suppressed wage rates. Many migrant workers find it very difficult to pay for the living expenses of their dependents if they too were to reside in the cities.

Under the rural land tenure system, each rural household is entitled to the lease of a piece of collectively owned village farmland for 30 or more years. A farmer may sublease the farmland to other farmers but is not allowed to sell or mortgage the land individually since the farmer does not hold the land's full property right. Settling in a city by acquiring an urban *hukou* typically ends a farmer-migrant's membership of the rural collective that owns the farmland.

Unable to sell or mortgage the land, rural migrant workers have to remain rooted in their homeland to keep their entitlement to the land tenure. To a migrant worker, the leasehold at home village serves as a last-resort social safety net. Therefore, most migrant workers leave behind their junior or elder dependents to maintain their roots and keep their entitlement to the land. After working in the urban areas in their prime age, they will eventually return to their rural homeland where they become aged dependents themselves.

The New Normal

To understand the impact of demographics on income growth, we can apply the approach introduced by Aoki to decompose the sources of per capita income growth from the supply side.[6] By definition, per capita income can be decomposed as:

$$\text{Per capita income} = \frac{output}{population}$$

$$= \frac{output}{workers} \times \frac{workers}{working\text{-}age\ population}$$

$$\times \frac{working\text{-}age\ population}{population}$$

$$= labour\ productivity \times employment\ ratio$$

$$\times working\text{-}age\ population\ ratio$$

[6]Aoki Masahiko, "The Five-Phases of Economic Development and Institutional Evolution in China and Japan", *ADBI Working Paper Series*, no. 340, 2011.

Aoki further decomposes labour productivity as

labour productivity = (1 − *labour productivity gap between
urban and rural sector* × *rural share of
employment*) × *urban-sector labour
productivity*

The items inside the brackets measure the structural effects of urbanisation. Thus the growth of per capita income can be decomposed into:

Per capita income annual growth = *annual change of structural
effects* + *urban-sector
labour productivity growth
+ annual change of
employment ratio + annual
change of working-age
population ratio*

Aoki defines the first term as "Kuznets effect", which measures how urbanisation of rural labourers affects output. The analytical framework of the Aoki model also allows us to identify how much urban labour productivity is driven by a rise in capital intensity of production and how much is contributed by total factor productivity (TFP) growth in the urban sector.[7]

Applying the Aoki approach to official data, I decomposed China's per capita GDP growth since 1996 as displayed in Table 3 and Figure 13. From the results, it is clear that per capita income was mainly driven by the urban sector's labour productivity growth, which made up 6.04% of the average 8.71% annual growth of per capita GDP over the past 20 years. A main driver of urban-sector labour productivity growth was the urban-sector TFP growth. The other driver of labour productivity was the rise in capital intensity of production.

---

[7]Interested readers can refer to Aoki Masahiko, "The Five-Phases of Economic Development and Institutional Evolution in China and Japan", for technical details.

Table 3:   Decomposition of Per Capita GDP Growth

Five-Year Plan Period	Years	Per Capita GDP	Employment Ratio	Working-age Population Ratio	Kuznets Effect	Urban Labour Productivity	Urban Total Factor Productivity
9th	1996–2000	7.64%	–0.61%	0.87%	1.48%	5.82%	2.21%
10th	2001–2005	9.10%	–0.41%	0.54%	2.63%	6.18%	2.58%
11th	2006–2010	10.76%	–0.78%	0.68%	3.16%	7.47%	3.16%
12th	2011–2015	7.35%	0.28%	–0.41%	2.70%	4.66%	0.04%
Mean	1996–2015	8.71%	–0.38%	0.42%	2.49%	6.04%	2.00%
% of growth	1996–2015	100%	–4.37%	4.82%	28.63%	69.29%	

Source: Author's calculation.

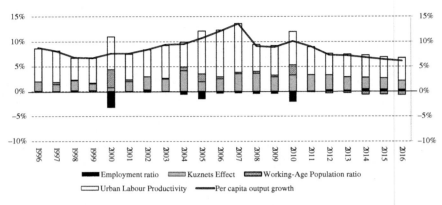

Figure 13:   Sources of Per capita GDP Growth (1996–2016)

Source: Author's calculation.

The second contributor to growth was the Kuznets effect, or urbani-sation of (rural) labour, which accounted for 2.5% annual growth in these two decades. Its role became more significant only since 2003 when the central government terminated the old practice of forcefully deporting rural migrants without work permit from the urban areas.

For most years since the turn of the century, the annual changes of employment ratio were negative, shaving off an average annual rate of −0.38% from per capita GDP growth. Note that employment ratio consists of labour participation rate and employment rate of labour force:

$$Employment\ Ratio = \frac{workers}{working\text{-}age\ population}$$

$$= \frac{workers}{labour\ force} \times \frac{labour\ force}{working\text{-}age\ population}$$

$$= employment\ rate\ of\ labour\ force$$

$$\times labour\ participation\ rate$$

In fact, the annual changes of employment rate and labour force par-ticipation rate were on average −0.10% and −0.28% respectively over these years. The long-term downward trend of labour participation rate has been well-documented in the literature.[8] It may be partially due to young adults taking more years in full-time schooling and partially as a result of rising affordability of early retirement or full-time homemaking.

A notable factor is the change in working-age population. Before 2010, its role in growth had been positive, adding on average 0.7% annually to per capita GDP growth from 1996 to 2010. Since 2011, however, its role has been reversed, deducting on average 0.4% per year from per capita GDP growth. The timing of losing the demographic dividends is consistent with the turning trends of working-age population and dependency ratios described in Figures 1 and 2.

The recent-year slowdown of per capita GDP growth thus can be attributed to three factors: the slower labour productivity growth, the weaker Kuznets effect and the shrinking labour force (Figure 13), all of which will continue to pose challenges to future economic growth.

After passing the Lewis turning point, the Kuznets effect is expected to diminish further, as the growth of rural migrant labour force becomes stagnant (Figure 6). According to the United Nations' projection, the working-age population ratio is projected to fall faster, taking away −0.67% from annual per capita GDP growth in the next five years. Labour productivity growth is likely to slow further given the sharp slowdown of TFP growth in the past few years (Table 3). High investment rate that has supported rapid capital accumulation and rise in capital intensity is becoming less sustainable in future,[9] especially with the rapid rise of an ageing population and elderly dependency ratios (Figure 2). That will weaken the other driver of labour productivity growth. The long-term downward trend of labour participation rate will also continue to pull the employment ratio down.

---

[8] Feng Shuaizhang, Hu Yingyao and Robert Moffitt, "Long Run Trends in Unemployment and Labor Force Participation in China", *NBER Working Paper*, no. 21460, 2015.

[9] Cai Fang and Lu Yang, "Population Change and Resulting Slowdown in Potential GDP Growth in China", *China & World Economy*, vol. 21, no. 2, 2013, pp. 1–14.

Final Remarks

In summary, China's demographic transition has passed a turning point where the past bonus has been exhausted and the future onus is unfolding. This demographic impact will cast a long shadow on the prospect of economic growth in the coming years and even decades. Meanwhile, there are signs that the rural-urban labour migration has also passed the Lewis turning point. The supply of rural surplus labour, which has provided the basis of the country's formidable comparative advantages in labour-intensive manufacturing products, is becoming less abundant and drying up quickly. On top of that, the pattern of migration of rural workers is featured by "youth drain", contributing to interregional and rural-urban disparity. Given the accumulated effects of "youth drain", most of the rural, in-land and poor regions have already lost demographic dividends earlier than the urban, coastal and richer regions. The demographics are therefore not favourable for late-and-less developed areas to catch up with the more developed ones in the future.

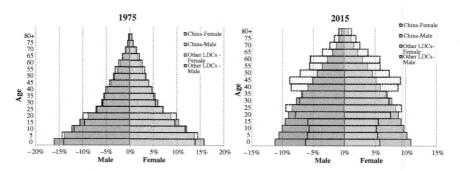

Figure 14: Population Age Structure: China versus Other Less Developed Countries

Note: Other LDCs (less developed countries) refer to all regions of Africa, Asia (excluding Japan and China), Latin America and the Caribbean plus Melanesia, Micronesia and Polynesia.

Source: Compiled from United Nations, *World Population Prospects*.

Finally, from a global perspective, China's demographic structure, which was similarly young compared to the rest of the developing world 40 years ago, has now evolved to a much more aged one similar to those of rich and developed nations at the phase of post-demographic transition (Figure 14). The unfolding ageing society will relentlessly pressure the economy to upgrade its industrial structure to remain competitive in the global economy.

Index

agricultural liberalisation, 135, 139
agricultural reform, 131
Asian financial crisis, 7, 17, 38
Asian Infrastructure Investment Bank, 179
asset management, 142–143, 150, 154

Beibu Gulf Economic Zone, 179–180
Beijing–Tianjin–Hebei Economic Zone, 173, 177–178
Belt and Road initiatives, 4
    See also One Belt, One Road (OBOR)
bonds market, 5, 65–66, 75, 80
business tax, 85, 87–90, 94–95, 100

China dream, 177–178
    see also Chinese dream
China Securities Regulatory Commission (CSRC), 70–71
Chinese dream, 26
    see also China dream
collectively owned enterprises (COEs), 44
commercial banks, 30, 41, 65–69, 76

coordinated regional development, 176, 180–181
corporate governance, 36, 143, 149, 151, 153
Cultural Revolution, 45, 128, 131, 138, 190

demographic dividend, 9, 21, 164, 203, 212, 221–222
demographic transition, 201, 203, 222–223
Deng Xiaoping, 15, 171
deposit insurance, 68–70, 80

East Asian economies, 8–9, 15, 22
economic growth, 1–2, 4, 7–8, 12–13, 15–20, 23, 28, 34, 40, 83–85, 98, 108, 111, 113–114, 117, 124–125, 132, 171, 175, 179, 183, 185, 187, 189–191, 193, 195, 197, 200–204, 206, 221–222
economic restructuring, 2, 5, 22, 110, 113, 158, 173, 175
economic slowdown, 2, 17–19, 120
economic transformation, 5, 114, 117, 158–159

elderly dependency ratio, 205,
213–214, 221
equipment manufacturing, 4, 158,
161–162, 165
exchange rate regime, 5, 27, 40–41, 77

family planning, 190, 192, 203
fiscal capacity, 83–86, 91–92, 127,
138–139
of local governments, 84–86,
91–92
Five-Year Plan (Five-Year Programme),
85, 88, 111, 126, 157–158, 163,
165, 177, 181
13th Five-Year Plan, 85, 88, 111,
157–158, 163, 177, 181
food accessibility, 128, 132, 135–136,
138–140
food availability, 128, 136–139
food security, 5, 127–128, 132–133,
136–140
food supply, 128–130, 132, 136
foreign direct investment (FDI), 38,
125
formal sectors, 44, 57

Gini ratio, 15
global financial crisis, 7, 12, 14,
37–38, 77, 79, 113, 120
"Go Global" strategy, 4
grain circulation system, 128, 130, 135
grain reserves, 5, 127–128, 132–133,
135–136, 139–140
government subsidies, 44, 53–54, 63
central, 54, 63
local, 54
Great Famine, 128, 190
Great Western Development, 174

gross domestic product (GDP), 1, 3, 8,
10–12, 14–16, 18–19, 24–26, 32,
34, 41, 58–61, 83–86, 98–101, 107,
109, 111, 114–118, 120, 124–126,
171–172, 175, 181, 183–184, 190,
206, 209, 218–221
growth pattern, 18, 24, 200

high-speed railways, 179
household registration system, 119,
206–207, 216
see also *hukou* registration system
housing, 5, 15, 30, 91, 97–109
affordability, 99, 121
boom, 97–99
development, 97–98, 101, 104,
106–110
financing, 100
market, 97–99, 104–105, 109,
120–121, 191
marketisation, 97, 107,
109–110
mortgage, 91
reform, 97, 108–109
housing development, 97–98, 101,
104, 106–110
central government's role, 101,
106, 108–110
local governments' role, 100–103,
106–111
Housing Provident Fund, 100
housing wealth effect, 120, 122
Hu Jintao, 157, 175–177
hukou registration system, 100, 119,
206–207, 215–217
see also household registration
system
hyper growth, 2, 8–9, 12

income inequality, 15, 84, 91, 99, 140
industrial overcapacity, 14
industrial upgrading, 6, 14, 16, 22, 157, 175
innovation-driven, 4, 158–159, 175, 185
interest rate, 18, 28, 30–33, 35–38, 40–41, 52, 57, 60, 65–70, 76, 80, 99–100
interest rate corridor, 35–37
interest rate liberalisation, 31, 35, 66–70, 80
International Monetary Fund (IMF), 1, 8, 40, 77–80

Kuznets effect, 208, 218–221

labour productivity growth, 24, 163, 212, 218, 221
labour shortage, 6, 9, 22, 187–188, 191, 193
labour supply, 9, 188–189, 191–194, 199–200, 205, 209–210
land supply, 100
Leung Chun-ying, 73
Lewis turning point, 9, 205, 221–222
Li Keqiang, 3–4, 17–18, 23, 65, 70–71, 113, 158, 177
liquidity, 29–31, 35, 37, 39–41, 69, 119
liquidity constraints, 119
loss-making firms, 148

macroeconomic inbalance, 14
macroeconomic policies, 17
macroeconomic stability, 37, 41, 160
Made in China 2025, 5, 23, 157–161, 164–167

marketisation, 31, 66, 78, 97, 107, 109–110, 114, 130–131, 138–139
of renminbi (RMB), 78
of grain circulation, 130–131, 138–139
of interest rates, 31
exchange rate, 66
middle class, 121–124
migrant workers, 46, 119, 206, 209–210, 212, 216–217
Ministry of Human Resources and Social Security of China, 210–212
mixed ownership reform, 152–153, 156
modern services, 159
monetary autonomy, 38, 40
monetary policy, 3, 5, 27–28, 31–34, 36–42, 68, 120
money supply, 24, 28–29, 32, 38–39, 41

new normal, 2, 7, 17, 19, 23, 26, 110–111, 113, 157, 160, 183, 217

One Belt, One Road (OBOR), 177–180
see also Belt and Road initiatives
one-child policy, 4, 44, 55, 59, 100, 120, 187–188, 190–191, 193–196, 203
open-door policy, 7

Pay-as-you-go (PAYG), 43, 46, 59
Pearl River Delta region, 22, 173, 180
pension accounts, 45
People's Bank of China (PBOC), 27–41, 68, 78–79
population ageing, 6, 44, 54–55, 59, 119, 192, 195, 201

population decline, 196
population policy, 6, 187, 191, 196, 199
private consumption, 5, 113, 118, 122–125

quantitative credit, 28

regional development, 6, 106–107, 111, 171, 173–174, 176–181
regional disparity, 171, 180, 201
regional economic disparity, 6, 171–173, 176, 180
regional policy, 171, 174
research and development (R&D), 4, 16, 19–20, 163, 168
retirement ages, 61–62
rural social security system, 43, 46, 52, 56
rural-urban migration, 59, 206, 210, 212

saving rate, 14–15, 117, 120
Securities and Futures Commission (SFC), 70–72
shadow banking, 31–32, 34, 65, 67–69
Shenzhen–Hong Kong Stock Connect scheme, 73
Silk Road Fund, 179
social housing, 30, 101, 104, 107, 111
social pooling account, 43–46, 51–52, 54, 56, 58–61
social security contribution rate, 58, 61
social security debt, 46, 59–60
social security payment, 57, 61, 63

social security reforms, 43–44, 52, 59
social security system, 43–46, 51–56, 58–60, 62–63, 154
    rural, 43–44, 46, 52–53, 56, 62
    urban, 44, 47–53
special drawing rights (SDR), 40, 66, 77–81
state capital management, 143, 154
State-owned Assets Supervision and Administration Commission (SASAC), 142–143, 146–147, 150, 152, 154–155
state-owned enterprises, 3, 19, 21, 28, 31–32, 44–45, 58, 61, 67, 97, 125, 141, 147, 184
stock connect scheme, 66, 71, 73, 80
strategic emerging industries, 4, 157–158, 165, 170
structural reforms, 2, 16, 18–20, 32
supply-side policies, 18–20
sustainable development, 4, 173, 181

tax administration, 85, 88, 93–94, 96
tax system, 83–85, 88, 93
total factor productivity (TFP), 20–21, 218, 221
total fertility rate, 187–188, 191–193, 195, 202
transportation, 107, 175, 179–180
two-child policy, 188–189, 192, 194, 196, 199

urban resident social security programmes, 54
urbanisation, 16, 59, 107, 119–120, 123, 179, 206, 209–210, 218, 220

value added tax (VAT), 84–85, 87–90,
94–95

Wen Jiabao, 14, 157, 175
World Bank, 23–25, 62, 192, 194

Xi Jinping, 3, 16–20, 23, 26, 110,
171, 176–177

Yangtze River Delta region, 22, 173,
177–178
youth drain, 8, 201, 212–213, 215,
222

Zhu Rongji, 17